Teaching Systematic Synthetic Phonics and Early English

CRITICAL TEACHING

You might also like the following books in our *Critical Teaching* series

Beyond Early Reading
Edited by David Waugh and Sally Neaum
978-1-909330-41-2
In print

Inclusive Primary Teaching: A Critical Approach to Equality and Special Educational Needs
By Janet Goepel, Helen Childerhouse and Sheila Sharpe
978-1-909330-29-0
In print

Practical Ideas for Teaching Primary Science
By Vivian Cooke and Colin Howard
978-1-909682-29-0
In print

Primary School Placements: A Critical Guide to Outstanding Teaching
By Catriona Robinson, Branwen Bingle and Colin Howard
978-1-909330-45-0
In print

Reflective Primary Teaching
By Tony Ewens
978-1-909682-17-7
In print

Teaching and Learning Early Years Mathematics: Subject and Pedagogic Knowledge
By Mary Briggs
978-1-909330-37-5
In print

Understanding and Enriching Problem Solving in Primary Mathematics
By Patrick Barmby, David Bolden and Lynn Thompson
978-1-909330-69-6
In print

Most of our titles are also available in a range of electronic formats. To order please go to our website www.criticalpublishing.com or contact our distributor, NBN International, 10 Thornbury Road, Plymouth PL6 7PP, telephone 01752 202301 or email orders@nbninternational.com.

Teaching Systematic Synthetic Phonics and Early English

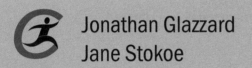

Jonathan Glazzard

Jane Stokoe

CRITICAL
TEACHING

First published in 2013 by Critical Publishing Ltd
Reprinted in 2014

British Library Cataloguing in Publication Data
A CIP record for this book is available from the British Library

ISBN: 978-1-909330-09-2

This book is also available in the following e-book formats:

MOBI ISBN: 978-1-909330-10-8
EPUB ISBN: 978-1-909330-11-5
Adobe e-book ISBN: 978-1-909330-12-2

Cover design by Greensplash Limited
Project Management by Out of House Publishing
Printed and bound in Great Britain by Bell & Bain, Glasgow

Critical Publishing
152 Chester Road
Northwich
CW8 4AL
www.criticalpublishing.com

MIX
Paper from
responsible sources
FSC
www.fsc.org   FSC® C013056

Contents

Meet the authors

Jonathan Glazzard
Jane Stokoe

Jonathan Glazzard is responsible for primary teacher training for early years and primary courses at the University of Huddersfield. Prior to this he worked as a primary school teacher, predominantly teaching in the Foundation Stage and Key Stage 1. He is passionate about promoting creative approaches to teaching which inspire both practitioners and children.

Jane Stokoe is a deputy headteacher in a Barnsley primary school. She is an experienced teacher and mentor of Initial Teacher Training students and she contributes to the primary programmes at the University of Huddersfield. She has been teaching for 35 years.

Introduction

There can be no more important subject than English in the school curriculum. English is a pre-eminent world language, it is at the heart of our culture and it is the language medium in which most of our pupils think and communicate. Literacy skills are also crucial to pupils' learning in other subjects across the curriculum.

(Ofsted, 2012a)

The government has demonstrated a clear commitment to raising attainment and achievement in all aspects of English. To accomplish this there is a need for a strong drive to ensure that all teachers understand both the theory and practice that will result in the best possible outcomes for all learners.

Too many pupils fail to meet the expected standards of attainment in communication, language and literacy by the end of Key Stage 1. Additionally one in five pupils are performing below the expected standards in English at the end of Key Stage 2. These issues are highlighted in the 2012 Ofsted report (Ofsted 2012a) *Moving English Forward: Action to Raise Standards in English*. Despite a rise in the proportion of children leaving the Early Years Foundation Stage with secure attainment in communication, language and literacy, there remains a minority of children who do not reach the expected levels of attainment. Systematic approaches are essential to support children in developing effective communication skills. These are pre-requisite skills which will enable children to become effective readers and writers.

Outstanding teaching impacts positively on outcomes for all learners. Teaching needs to be well planned to meet the diverse needs of pupils and be based on accurate assessments of prior achievement. As a trainee teacher you need to have a secure understanding of progression within all strands of English and you will need to adopt a systematic approach to enable children to make progress. Your training should provide you with a combination of theoretical and practical opportunities to develop your subject knowledge. You have a responsibility to reflect rigorously on your own strengths but most importantly your weaknesses and to take action to address these. This book will not guarantee that you will become an outstanding teacher of English. It will help you to further develop your knowledge, skills and understanding, but this will only become meaningful when you have rich opportunities and a drive to apply this learning in practical contexts.

Highly effective teachers of English understand that effective lessons must have good pace. However, providing children with too many activities in a given window of time will not result in effective learning. Children need sufficient time to work independently and to complete tasks in lessons. Learning is richer and deeper if children have a clear and measurable understanding of what constitutes success in any given task. Effective teaching is supported by powerful modelling of the processes of speaking, listening, reading and writing. However, it is your responsibility to ensure that they have adequate time within lessons to complete tasks to apply and demonstrate their own learning. Children need opportunities to become immersed in rich literacy activities through drama, discussion, debate, writing and reading. The importance of reading and writing for different purposes is vital in developing effective readers and writers and it is your responsibility to foster a love of books in children.

You should maximise the time for children to apply and consolidate learning. You need to plan creative lessons which excite and engage learners. You need to place your lessons within a context so that children are presented with learning that is both stimulating and has a clear purpose. Planning clear sequences of lessons which focus on developing specific skills, knowledge and understanding is an essential pre-requisite for effective independent learning. You would not be able to drive a car without specifically being taught the skills to do so. Children equally are disadvantaged if they have not been taught the skills of reading, writing and communication.

The Ofsted report (2012b) *From Training to Teaching Early Language and Literacy* highlights that some trainees and newly qualified teachers have insufficient knowledge about progression in learning as well as an inability to make adaptations to meet the many differing needs of children. Your training should provide you with the experience of teaching all aspects of English and you should have experience of teaching a range of age groups. Additionally, your training should provide you with practical experiences of teaching literacy to learners with special educational needs and/or disabilities, those with English as an Additional Language and those who are more able. You should have opportunities to observe outstanding teachers of English. Where these experiences are not evident you should seek support from your training provider to address the gaps in your subject and pedagogical knowledge. It is fundamental that you understand the relationship between communication, language, reading and writing. All areas of English are inter-related and of equal importance.

Since the publication of the independent review of the teaching of reading (Rose, 2006), training providers have been challenged by the government and by Ofsted to ensure that they provide trainees with high-quality training in Systematic Synthetic Phonics. The quality of central provision in this aspect has subsequently improved and this should provide you with a secure basis for teaching early reading and writing. The challenge for providers is to ensure that school-based training in Systematic Synthetic Phonics is of a high standard so that you benefit significantly from high-quality provision in schools. Inevitably the teaching of English is of variable quality in schools, but outcomes for children will not improve unless teaching is at least good or outstanding. There is still too much teaching that is of satisfactory quality. We hope that this book will inspire you to teach good and outstanding lessons, but it needs to be supplemented with opportunities for you to work with inspirational teachers within schools.

Children will not be motivated to read or write unless they are presented with contexts that are stimulating, and learning will be disconnected if elements of English are taught in isolation without connection to a central theme. The National Strategies worked hard to provide teachers with materials to further enhance their subject knowledge. Many of the materials produced were excellent and provided teachers and trainees with a secure knowledge and understanding of all aspects of English. However, the National Strategies have also left their legacy in the form of unit plans, which although useful in some respects, can result in teaching which lacks context, purpose or connection to the other learning undertaken in classrooms.

We hope that you will be passionate about the teaching of English. We hope that you will understand the importance of providing your learners with rich, practical first-hand experiences within all aspects of English. Our view is that most learners will not be motivated by repetitive tasks and written exercises which focus on grammar, spelling and punctuation. We have concerns that the draft National Curriculum proposals for English may result in teachers over-focusing on the technical aspects of writing rather than on the development of children's creative ideas. We urge trainees and teachers to keep creativity central to their philosophy of education. We support the 'Talk for Writing' project and in particular the concept of oral rehearsal prior to writing.

As a teacher you have an important role to play in empowering children to believe that they can be speakers, listeners, readers and authors. Once they believe this, you will be able to focus on improving the quality of their outputs. The process of learning is just as important as the final product, and children need to be encouraged to experiment with ideas and to work collaboratively to share ideas. Creating a positive classroom ethos where learners feel empowered to work in a collaborative way is an important role of the educator. In developing as speakers, listeners, readers and writers, children need focused targets on a step-by-step basis. Giving them too many targets will overwhelm them and lead to a sense of failure. You need to ensure that your learners understand the importance of communication and of being literate, and their relevance to the wider world in which they live. Communication, language and literacy are fundamental because they unlock the door to learning across the curriculum. All children are entitled to high-quality teaching which stimulates, excites and empowers learners to be lifelong speakers, listeners, readers and writers. You have a duty to ensure that you fulfil your responsibilities in this respect.

1 Oral development in the early years

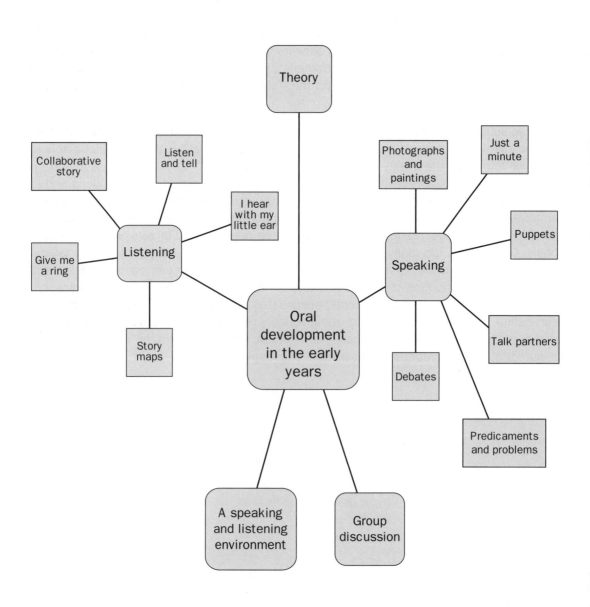

Links to the Early Years Foundation Stage

Communication and language: Listening and attention

By the end of the Early Years Foundation Stage, children should be able to listen attentively in a range of situations.

Communication and language: Understanding

By the end of the Early Years Foundation Stage, children should be able to follow instructions and answer questions about stories or events.

Communication and language: Speaking

By the end of the Early Years Foundation Stage, children should be able to express themselves effectively using past, present and future forms. They should be able to develop their oral narratives and explanations by connecting ideas.

Literacy: Reading and writing

By the end of the Early Years Foundation Stage children should be able to understand simple sentences.

Links to the National Curriculum

The National Curriculum emphasises the importance of speaking and listening and their role in supporting the development of reading and writing.

The theory

Theories of language development help to explain how children acquire language. Language acquisition is a pre-requisite skill for good oral communication and understanding. Behaviourist theories (eg B.F. Skinner) assume that language is acquired through a combination of imitation and conditioning. These theories argue that as soon as children begin to use recognisable language they are rewarded with a positive response from the adults around them. This response results in them repeating the language that they hear around them. Biological or nativist theories (eg Chomsky) assume that children are born with an innate language acquisition device (LAD) which enables them to develop language. They believe that the language children hear is insufficient to enable them to access language and that the brain is biologically programmed to enable children to use language at specific times. Interactionist theorists (eg Vygotsky) assume that language is acquired through a combination of factors including social interaction, biological, cultural and environmental influences.

Listening

You cannot assume that all children will use their listening skills effectively. As with all skills, listening skills need to be taught and then reinforced as children access the broader curriculum. As children listen, language is modelled to them. They will develop an understanding of the ways in which tone and volume as well as gesture support speakers in communicating meaning. Additionally, children will develop an understanding of the need to take turns in conversation, of how people in a group interact with one another and of the ways in which speech can impact on others. You will need to further develop children's listening skills by initially modelling the need to question what they have heard to further clarify their understanding. By taking turns in conversation children will also realise that they can build on what others have said. Children should be engaged in opportunities to demonstrate their understanding of what they have heard. You should also communicate to children that, when listening to others, non-verbal responses are useful tools in acknowledging what they have heard. Good eye contact with the speaker and body language that confirms that they are paying attention are acceptable responses and children may need to be explicitly taught these skills.

You must also encourage and support children to demonstrate that they have listened carefully and that they have gained meaning from what they have heard. You should ensure that children have opportunities to demonstrate that they have developed an overall understanding of what they have heard. Equally it is important to ensure that they can recall the key events and ideas that have been communicated to them. You can assess their understanding in several different ways including asking them to present the information again in their own words. When children have listened to instructions, you must assess that they are able to follow them. Check that children's responses to what they have heard are relevant and encourage them to ask questions to further support their understanding. Children should not be simply expected to listen but should be encouraged and supported to maintain communication with others. Listening to and responding to others will be beneficial in developing children's understanding and use of language.

A number of activities will support you in developing effective listening skills with your children.

Listen and tell

Your children will need to listen carefully as you tell them a new story. You will then ask the children, each working with a partner, to retell the story they have heard. The retelling should contain as much detail as possible. One of the children should begin to retell the story to their partner. On a given signal the second child continues to retell the story from the point at which the first child has stopped. This turn-taking sequence continues until the story is complete. As the children work, you must listen carefully, noting their ability to recall the events of the story in sequence, the story plot and the use of some story language, although you would not expect children to use exactly the same words used in the original story. They need to listen carefully to both the story and to their partner to continue the story.

I hear with my little ear

In this game, children are totally reliant upon what they hear and have no visual cues to support them. Again this is a useful activity for children working in pairs. The speaker (one of the children) must communicate clear information, while the listener is only able to ask questions to further clarify their understanding. This activity can be used in a range of ways, and the following is only one example of the effective use of this strategy. The children should sit on either side of a screen or back-to-back. The speaker carefully describes an object and as he does so the listener must draw what is described. The aim of the game is for the listener to identify the object that the speaker has described.

Collaborative story

In this activity a story is developed with a partner or a group of peers. In partner work, the first child must verbalise either a word or a phrase which the partner then adds to. The children continue taking turns to add either a single word or phrase to create a story. In this activity, children are required to listen carefully to one another so that they can ensure that the story they have created makes sense.

Story maps

In this activity, children will illustrate the key events in a story. You will begin to read a story, emphasising that the children must listen carefully. At a specific point in the story you stop and give children time to illustrate what they have heard. Continue and stop again so that the children can add further illustrations. For young children it is beneficial to present them with a simple blank story map to ensure that the illustrations are drawn in the correct order. At the end of the story-telling, you should engage the children in retelling the story by referring to their drawings.

Give me a ring

As you introduce children to this activity you must stress the importance of clear communication. The benefits of facial expressions and body language will be withdrawn and understanding will be heavily reliant upon the use of language and effective listening skills. This activity is particularly successful when carried out with a partner. The children sit back-to-back and take turns in discussing a topic or event. They must listen carefully to one another, respond to one another and take turns in conversation.

As the teacher, it is your role to communicate to children the importance of listening. You must not fall into the trap of repeating what children say. In an effective listening environment, children will understand that they should listen carefully to others in order for them to respond to what has been said without it being reiterated by you. It is too easy to repeat to others what a child has said, but in effect doing so confirms that listening is optional. Additionally, the teacher should avoid repeating teaching points or instructions to the class since there should be an understanding that all children should be listening the first time. Children often do not hear what speakers are saying because their peers may be speaking inaudibly. When children are speaking they need to be taught to speak in a clear, audible voice and this in turn will facilitate effective listening.

When communicating with children do not be tempted to raise your voice to be heard. Speak in a clear, audible voice which can be heard by children who are listening. The children in your class may respond to questions with vague statements. This is often because they have not listened carefully to the question. Children need to be taught about the vocabulary associated with questions which often begin with *what, how, why, who* and *when*. They need to be taught to listen carefully to ensure that their responses are relevant.

As a teacher, it is your role to plan listening activities across the curriculum that have a clear purpose. As you communicate with children you should also model effective listening skills by ensuring that you maintain good eye contact, ask questions and respond to the speaker using verbal and non-verbal cues. Children will need to practise these strategies and should be engaged in assessing their own listening skills.

Speaking

The skill of speaking is central to oracy, and children need to be able to articulate their thoughts before they can write. Children who are able to *say* a sentence will find it easier to *write* a sentence. Additionally, through speaking, children will be able to practise using an increasingly wide range of vocabulary that they will be able to use in their writing. The more children read, the wider their vocabulary will be and this will improve the quality of their oral outputs. Children who listen to others will develop a wider vocabulary which they can draw on to improve the quality of their own speaking and writing.

You need to understand the inter-relationship between speaking, listening, reading and writing and you need to plan for speaking opportunities in the classroom in the same way that you plan for and value reading and writing. You should not assume that speaking will happen incidentally, and you will need to provide a speaking curriculum in which talk is valued as an output. Too often teachers feel pressurised into getting children to produce written outputs. A piece of writing produces tangible evidence of children's progress and can be used to support assessment judgements, whereas children's talk is often under-valued, perhaps because it cannot be stored in a file and produced as evidence during school inspections. However, you can capture children's talk by audio-recording or even filming children while they are talking. This evidence can then be used to support your assessments of children's speaking and listening skills.

Children need to be able to adapt their speaking to a range of listeners. In the early stages of development they need to understand the difference between the way they might speak in informal situations, such as the playground, and the way they are expected to speak in the classroom. As children develop further they need to understand that they will need to modify the way they speak depending on who they are talking to.

Children should be encouraged to use talk to develop their thinking and reasoning. Talk is a powerful cross-curricular tool for children to use in different subjects. They can use talk to orally rehearse their writing by talking through their ideas with a partner prior to the writing process. Additionally, in mathematics they can talk through mathematical problems with a talk partner before being expected to make a response. This is a very useful strategy during whole-class sessions and allows children additional thinking time before they answer a question. You will need to make decisions about how you pair children in these situations. Pairing a less able child with a more able child can be beneficial because the more able child can scaffold the learning of the less able child. However, mixed ability grouping can lead to more able children dominating talk and becoming frustrated. It is probably more effective to vary the pairings so that children work with different talk partners throughout the year. Before planning a science investigation in small groups, children can use talk to clarify their ideas and to agree how they will carry out the investigation. In history, children can use talk to discuss historical source material including artefacts, pictures and photographs. They could use talk to ask questions to visiting guests who have been invited into the classroom to share their expertise. In drama, children can use talk to express themselves in pairs and small groups. The possibilities for using talk are endless but you need to recognise the ways in which talk is a powerful tool for learning across the curriculum. It is not something that is confined to English lessons and you need to value talk as a valid learning output across the breadth of the curriculum in the same way that written outputs are valued.

CASE STUDY

Ameera was teaching an English lesson on the Victorians to a small group of children aged five to six. She had brought in a collection of Victorian artefacts for the children to explore. These included an old iron, a washtub and mangle, and some clothing. The children enjoyed talking about the artefacts and handling them. Ameera started the lesson by asking the children to think of questions to ask about the artefacts. The remainder of the lesson was spent using the washtub to wash one of the items of clothing followed by using the mangle. The children were very engaged throughout the lesson. The mentor observed the lesson and provided Ameera with feedback at the end of the lesson. She graded the lesson as satisfactory because the children did not produce any writing about their learning. Ameera had not made any explicit links to speaking and listening on her lesson plan. Instead she had identified links to history and writing.

- Do you think the rationale for the judgement on the lesson was fair?
- How might Ameera modify her planning if she was going to repeat this lesson?

Speaking cannot be a valued output for learning if children are expected to learn in silence. Your classroom should be a busy place in which talking is promoted and nurtured. Children need opportunities to speak to others in pairs, small groups and whole-class situations. They need opportunities to speak in both formal and informal situations, and as children become more confident they need to use sustained talk by speaking for extended periods of time. Adults play a fundamental role in scaffolding children's talk. In the Early Years Foundation Stage, adults can play alongside children and introduce children to an increasingly wide range of vocabulary. Very young children are capable of using and understanding quite sophisticated vocabulary if it is powerfully modelled.

CASE STUDY

Jebar was teaching a lesson which focused on vocabulary development to a class of Reception children. He took in a collection of objects, which he had found in his garage, in a large sack. He started the lesson by explaining that he had been clearing out his garage at the weekend, and started to pull the items out of the sack one at a time. As he introduced the various items, he used words such as *dirty*, *smelly* and *old*. Then he pulled out another item and introduced children to the word *fragile*. He explained the meaning of this word by demonstrating how the object had a crack running through it. He then pulled out another object and used the word *dilapidated*. Again he explained the meaning of this word. Later Jebar overheard the children using some of these words in their own conversations.

*   How did Jebar maximise the opportunities for learning in this lesson?
*   Children need to hear words several times before they start to use them. What follow-on activities might be appropriate in this lesson to support the whole-class input?

Talk partners

We briefly mentioned this strategy earlier in this chapter. In this strategy, children are placed in pairs and allocated a specific amount of time to solve a problem, share ideas or generate solutions. It is important that children understand that each person should make an equal contribution, and unless this is managed carefully some children may dominate the discussions.

*   Consider what strategies you might put into place to ensure that children take turns.
*   How might you use this strategy across the curriculum?

Debates

Debates are a powerful way of introducing children to the notion that different people hold different opinions. They can also be used to introduce children to controversial topics. Children can be divided into two groups to debate an issue. It is useful to ask them to argue a specific point of view, so for example if they are debating whether animals should be kept in zoos one of the groups could be asked to present the reasons why zoos are necessary, and the other group could argue against zoos. Children need to be given time to orally rehearse their arguments and they need to be taught the skills of being an effective speaker and listener. These include turn-taking, not interrupting, valuing other people's opinions, listening to others and modifying opinions in light of discussions. The skill of debating needs to be modelled to children. A useful way of doing this is for the teacher and teaching assistant to model having a debate. We have carried out class debates with children in Year 2 and they have been very successful. However, you do need to find topics that children are interested in and can relate to and you should be aware of the implications of introducing children to highly sensitive issues.

Puppets

Puppets are a useful way of encouraging children to orally retell stories. They can be placed on an interactive display which gives children access to the text and to an audio-recording of the story. Children can then use the puppets to talk through the story, working in pairs or individually. They can be encouraged to use different voices for different characters.

Predicaments and problems

Presenting children with problems is a useful vehicle for developing children's talk. An easy way to do this is to read a story up to a point where a character needs to make a critical decision. The children can then use talk to discuss what the character should do next. As they talk they will need to weigh up conflicting points of view. This strategy can be applied using traditional stories. For example, children can discuss whether Red Riding Hood should walk through the woods and what the consequences might be. Paired improvisation is a useful way of implementing this technique. In this strategy, children will work in pairs, each taking on the role of a character. In the above example, one person could take on the role of Red Riding Hood's mother, and the other could take on the role of Red Riding Hood. The 'mother' will try to persuade Red Riding Hood to take the walk through the woods and, together, both will explore the consequences of either making the journey or staying at home. Eventually the problem will be solved and Red Riding Hood will decide which action to take.

Just a minute

This strategy focuses the children on talking for an extended period of time. In this case, a child is given a topic and asked to speak for one minute without deviation, hesitation or repetition. This is challenging and children need time to think through their ideas before they do this.

Photographs and paintings

Photographs and paintings can stimulate talk across the curriculum. However, it might be useful to structure children's talk in these instances by giving them a series of prompts or questions upon which to base their talk. Children's talk benefits from having a structure in a similar way to how their writing can be aided using writing frames.

- Consider how you might use photographs and paintings across the curriculum, to develop children's talk.

Children need access to good role models when developing their talk. As a teacher you should provide children with a good model of standard spoken English and this is now an expectation of the Teachers' Standards.

Group discussion

You must ensure that children have opportunities for planned discussion and interaction. This can be effectively facilitated by engaging them in opportunities to work together in pairs or small groups. By supporting them to work collaboratively and co-operatively you will be providing them with opportunities to develop their language and their social skills. By sharing ideas with others, children will further develop their own views and ideas as they acknowledge and respond to each other's contributions. They will also develop the skill of taking turns in conversations.

Children need to be engaged in discussion for a range of purposes which could include:

- investigating;
- problem-solving;
- planning;
- sorting;
- predicting;
- reporting;
- evaluating.

Through discussion, children will develop the ability to agree and disagree, to question and to reflect.

Young children gain much from the activity *think–pair–share*. In this activity they begin by considering their individual responses to a problem or an issue. Once they have done so, you invite them to explain their ideas to a partner. They then share their ideas with another pair of children. The expectation is that the final group will have reached a final viewpoint in relation to the problem or issue.

You should consider the following points in supporting children in developing the ability to benefit from group discussion.

- Initially focus on ensuring that children can listen and respond as individuals.

- Once they have developed the ability to respond on an individual basis, challenge them to work in pairs in which each child listens to the other and makes contributions.

- When paired work is secure, children will be ready to work in small groups without feeling intimidated or threatened.

The size of the group can be extended as children develop the confidence and skills to listen to others, build on what they are saying and challenge their perspectives. This will provide children with exposure to more ideas and viewpoints.

A speaking and listening environment

Speaking and listening opportunities can be facilitated through an effective learning environment which promotes talking and listening opportunities. An effective classroom environment may include:

- a speaking area which includes digital recorders for recording children's voices;

- a listening area which includes digital recorders for listening to stories and poems;

- interactive displays which include key questions to stimulate both thought and talk;

- play areas which facilitate social interaction and communication. Adults scaffold learning in these areas by playing alongside children and extending the breadth of their spoken vocabulary;

- a book area which includes a range of types of texts and comfortable seating, so that children can share stories and other texts together;

- a carpet area for class discussions, story time and circle time;

- props for story-telling including puppets, story boxes and small world play;

- furniture arranged to facilitate paired and group work;

- a role-play area linked to a class theme/topic;

- a computer area with headphones so that children can listen to talking books.

As a teacher you need to model the skills of speaking and listening. If you want children to be effective speakers and listeners you need to model that you listen to what they are telling you and you need to ensure that your interactions with other adults in the room provide powerful models of effective speaking and listening.

Critical questions

» *Can standard spoken English be used across all accents?*

» *What issues can arise when teachers' own accents are different to children's accents?*

» *What issues can arise in cases where children are taught standard spoken English in school but may not be exposed to standard spoken English at home?*

» *What is the impact of the home environment on children's speaking and listening skills?*

» *To what extent has the growth of modern technology influenced the development of children's speaking and listening skills?*

» *To what extent do teachers dominate classroom discussions?*

CREATIVE APPROACH

Precious was placed in a school that used the Kagan approach for her final block of school experience. The approach focuses on maximising pupil participation in lessons through the use of collaborative groups. In this school the use of Kagan strategies was embedded in all age groups and across all subjects. Children worked in ability groups in some lessons, and mixed-ability Kagan groups in other lessons. Each Kagan group consisted of four children representing the full ability spectrum. In one lesson, Precious wanted to focus the children on the use of powerful verbs to strengthen their writing.

At the start of the lesson, Precious told the children that they would be using powerful verbs to write a poem about fireworks. She flashed up some images of fireworks on the interactive whiteboard and subsequently asked the children to talk to their talk partners about their own experiences of fireworks. Precious then stopped the children after precisely two minutes and summarised their talk by giving examples of the powerful verbs she had heard them using. She then asked them to go to their Kagan groups to produce a mind map of powerful verbs to describe fireworks. Photographs of fireworks were scattered on the tables to stimulate the children's talk. Using large sheets of sugar paper and marker pens, the children then produced mind maps of words to describe fireworks. Examples of words used included *screeching, fizzing, popping* and *sizzling*.

After five minutes, Precious brought the class together and quickly modelled the process of writing an acrostic poem using shared writing as an approach. She modelled how to complete one line of the acrostic and then asked the class to work in talk partners to think of their own ideas for completing the second line. She stressed the point that each line had to include a powerful verb. She then asked the children to move into ability groups to complete their own acrostic poem. Different learning outcomes were specified for each group. However, the mind maps produced by the Kagan groups were available for children on the tables to support their writing.

In the middle of the lesson, Precious asked the children to complete a 'roam around the room'. They were required to move around the room and look at other people's writing. She asked them to find one powerful verb that another child had used for them to use in their own writing.

• How were the Kagan groups used to good effect in this lesson to maximise achievement for all children?

• Why do you think that Precious did not model writing the whole acrostic poem with the children?

• Why do you think that Precious did not ask the children to feed back their ideas after the initial talk partner activity?

• How was talk used in this lesson to scaffold the children's writing?

INTERNATIONAL PERSPECTIVES

In Denmark and Finland, there is a greater emphasis placed on oracy than in England for children at the age of six. In England, greater emphasis is placed on reading and writing at the expense of speaking and listening. However, by the age of 15, Finnish children outperform children in England, despite the fact that, at the age of six, children in England are further ahead than Finnish children in reading and writing.

Critical reflection

Critically consider the following questions.

» *To what extent has the standards agenda in primary schools in England led to the marginalisation of speaking and listening in the classroom?*

» *School inspections in England include work scrutiny of children's mathematics and literacy books. To what extent can this lead to the marginalisation of speaking and listening?*

Critical points

This chapter has emphasised the importance of:

» *providing children with planned opportunities to develop their speaking and listening skills;*

» *valuing speaking and listening so that they have the same status as reading and writing;*

» *planning opportunities to develop children's speaking and listening skills across the curriculum;*

» *talk in the writing process;*

» *developing children's vocabulary through a structured approach to teaching.*

Taking it further

Alexander, R.J. (2008) *Towards Dialogic Teaching: Rethinking Classroom Talk* (4th edn). York: Dialogos.

Waugh, D. and Jolliffe, W. (2008) *English 3–11: A Guide for Teachers*. Abingdon: Routledge.

2 Communication and language development in the early years

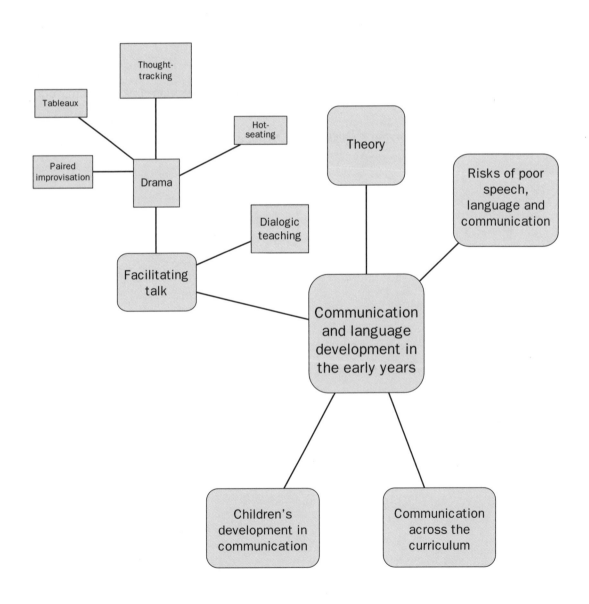

Links to the Early Years Foundation Stage

Communication and language: Listening and attention

By the end of the Early Years Foundation Stage, children should be able to listen attentively in a range of situations.

Communication and language: Understanding

By the end of the Early Years Foundation Stage, children should be able to follow instructions and answer questions about stories or events.

Communication and language: Speaking

By the end of the Early Years Foundation Stage, children should be able to express themselves effectively using past, present and future forms. They should be able to develop their oral narratives and explanations by connecting ideas.

Literacy: Reading and writing

By the end of the Early Years Foundation Stage, children should be able to understand simple sentences.

Links to the National Curriculum

The National Curriculum emphasises the importance of speaking and listening and their role in supporting the development of reading and writing.

The theory

Piaget emphasised that children initially start to use egocentric speech: at this stage, children have no interest in who they are speaking to and whether they are being listened to. Thus, children frequently talk in monologue and do not have conversations with others. Piaget argued that speech later becomes socialised. At this stage, children start to take account of what others say and use conversational speech in a variety of ways.

Vygotsky essentially believed that language is learned through social interaction with others. He believed that children's experiences with language are social from the outset rather than being egocentric. Vygotsky believed that social communication subsequently results in inner speech (internal dialogue) rather than the other way round. Thus, according to his theory, interactions on the social plane (social language) result in development on the individual plane (internal dialogues).

Chomsky believed that children are innately programmed to use and understand language through an internal language acquisition device (LAD) which enables them to master the structure of language. His theory assumes that there is no need for children to be taught language directly, providing they are immersed in an environment where language is used constantly (Palaiologou, 2010).

Bruner emphasised the role of the adult in scaffolding children's language development rather than the direct teaching of language.

Critical questions

»   *Can you find any critiques of these theories?*

»   *What are the implications of these theories?*

Children's development in communication

You cannot assume that children's speech, language and communication skills will develop automatically. As a teacher you play a fundamental role in supporting the development of these skills through your interactions with children and through creating an enabling learning environment which supports the development of language, talk and communication. Communication and language skills are the basis for children to subsequently become good readers and writers. It is essential that you have some understanding of typical levels of development so that you can identify children who need further support. Although children are unique individuals and develop at their own rates, benchmarking their development against typical development will enable you to identify those children who may be struggling, thus enabling you to provide targeted intervention to groups and individuals.

The Communication Trust (2011) provides some useful benchmarks for communication development and you can also refer to the Development Matters guidance in the Early Years Foundation Stage to help you identify what stages children have reached.

By *six months* babies usually:

*   make sounds, including crying, gurgling and babbling to themselves and others;
*   make noises to get your attention;
*   watch your face when you talk to them;
*   get excited when they hear voices, perhaps by kicking, waving their arms or making noises;
*   smile and laugh when other people laugh;
*   make sounds back when talked to.

(Communication Trust, 2011)

You can facilitate communication in babies by getting down to their level so that they can see your face. Talking to them and singing songs and rhymes are basic activities that should engender a response in babies. Using facial expressions and leaving gaps in your conversations to enable them to give a response are also useful strategies for facilitating communication.

By *one year of age*, children use a wider range of communication strategies. At this age they may point to get your attention and they begin to understand simple words, especially if these are accompanied with a gesture. At this age babies can usually:

*   recognise the names of familiar objects;
*   take turns in 'conversations' through babbling back to an adult;

- babble strings of sounds;

- say simple words.

(Communication Trust, 2011)

You can play with children at this age and use simple words and phrases to describe what is happening. Saying simple words and accompanying these with gestures also helps to aid vocabulary development.

By the *age of 18 months*, babies will usually attempt to talk, using a limited number of words. These words will be words that they have heard in the home. Some of the words may not be pronounced correctly and after they have spoken a word you can repeat it back to them so they can hear the correct articulation. It is at this age that children usually begin to understand simple phrases and they can usually recognise a wider range of objects than they are able to name. Extending children's vocabulary at this age is vital, so when children point to objects it is important to tell them the correct name of the object. As a teacher you need to model correct spoken English so you will need to use the correct words for objects. However, you will also need to bear in mind that parents may have introduced children to alternative 'baby' words and they will need to unlearn these.

By the *age of two*, children usually have a greater vocabulary. They understand and use more words and they use and understand a wider repertoire of short phrases. Children often understand more than they can say. Typically children at the age of two can:

- use 50 or more single words;

- use short phrases;

- ask simple questions;

- understand 200–500 words;

- understand simple questions;

- enjoy pretend play;

- become frustrated when they are unable to make themselves understood.

(Communication Trust, 2011)

You can extend their language development by using adjectives to describe simple nouns. Playing with children, extending their vocabulary and sharing books are essential activities for extending children's language and communication.

At the *age of three*, children will:

- use up to 300 words, including nouns and adjectives;

- use simple verbs;

- use simple prepositions;

- string four or five words together to say simple captions;

- ask questions;

- have clearer speech;

- understand longer instructions and questions;
- be able to have conversations.

(Communication Trust, 2011)

Children may have specific difficulties with the pronunciation of sounds such as 'sh', 'ch' and 'th' and they may miss sounds off the beginning of words. The most effective way of addressing this is to repeat back what they have said using the correct pronunciations of words. It is at this stage that you should be engaging children in extended conversations. Children may not speak in full sentences at the age of three. Rather than correcting them, it is better to repeat back what they have said using full sentences so that their self-concepts are not damaged.

By the *age of four*, children are usually able to:

- say many more words, phrases and sentences;
- use longer sentences and link sentences;
- use clearer speech;
- describe past events that they have experienced;
- listen to longer stories and answer simple questions about them;
- use words relating to number, colour and time;
- enjoy imaginative play.

(Communication Trust, 2011)

By the *age of five*, children will usually:

- take turns in much longer conversations;
- use correct sentences when speaking;
- understand the meanings of words;
- retell short stories in sequence;
- use most sounds of speech;
- enjoy listening to stories, songs and rhymes;
- understand spoken instructions;
- use talk to take on different roles in imaginative play;
- use talk to solve problems and organise thinking and activities;
- understand words such as *first*, *next*, *last* and simple prepositions.

(Communication Trust, 2011)

If you are teaching in a Reception class, some children may need specific targeted support with the pronunciation of certain speech sounds such as '*th*' or '*sh*'. As a prime area of learning in the Early Years Foundation Stage you need to create a learning environment which supports the development of communication and language. One of the fundamental skills that you need to develop in children is the skill of listening. Some children will have been raised in a home environment where parents have modelled good listening skills. However, some children may have been raised in environments where they have not been listened to and where adults do not listen to each other. As a teacher you need to model the skills of listening and attention by listening carefully to what children say. The skill of listening may need to be explicitly taught through a range of whole-class, group or paired activities. These may include:

- circle time games which require children to take turns speaking by passing round an object – only the person holding the object is permitted to speak;

- telephone activities where two people have a conversation using a pretend telephone;

- barrier games – two children are positioned facing each other with a barrier between them. One child instructs the other child on how to build a tower / sculpture using different coloured multilink cubes. As each instruction is given, the second child follows it. Instructions are kept simple such as *put a red cube on top of a blue cube*; *put a yellow cube underneath the green cube*. The end result should be two identical models.

- passing a story round a circle – *Grandma went to the shop and bought ...* Each child offers a contribution, but it must not be something that has already been offered.

During child-initiated independent activities, children need to be taught to listen to each other during their play. You may need to support children in doing this by playing alongside them and modelling the skills of listening and attention. During lessons, children may also need support in listening carefully to others and responding to what they say.

An enabling environment which facilitates listening and attention should include:

- a listening area where children can enjoy rhymes and stories;

- opportunities for children to listen to rhymes, stories and songs and join in with them;

- opportunities for children to share their experiences with others;

- songs that require turn-taking;

- use of puppets/props for retelling stories;

- use of sand timers to extend the concentration of children who find it difficult to focus their attention on a task.

The learning environment should be rich in talk. You should provide children with opportunities to initiate discussions and have conversations with each other. A rich play-based learning environment will facilitate opportunities for talk, communication and social interaction. Children should be provided with puppets, and props such as masks of characters from stories, to facilitate speaking as they re-enact scenes from well-known stories. Children should be provided with meaningful speaking and listening activities in a range of contexts. You should consider how to provide opportunities for children to use speaking and listening, language and communication in all areas of the curriculum. Communication and language are cross-curricular tools and you should plan for children to develop these skills in a range of contexts. As a teacher it is critical that you plan opportunities to develop children's vocabulary at this stage of their development. Playing alongside them in the sand, water and role-play areas will enable you to extend children's vocabulary by introducing them to new words. Curiosity areas can be created in the classroom using interesting materials and objects, and these provide rich opportunities for extending children's understanding and use of vocabulary. When planning for play-based learning you should think carefully about how play areas can be developed to extend children's use of language and vocabulary. It is too easy to take communication and language for granted, but a carefully planned learning environment will have a major impact on children's development in this area. Some children may not have had regular opportunities to communicate with adults at home and their skills may have been restricted due to over-exposure to television or computers. In some households, communication is restricted by such technological developments.

Critical questions

» *What are the beneficial and limiting effects of technological innovations on children's communication and language?*

» *How can practitioners support parents in developing communication-friendly spaces in the home environment?*

You need to be able to identify children who might be at risk of under-development in speech language and communication. Early identification and intervention will minimise subsequent under-achievement. These children may typically display:

• poor speech which is unclear in places;

• a limited understanding of words and phrases;

• a limited spoken vocabulary or an inability to connect words to form sentences;

• an inability or limited ability to use language in social situations;

• lack of fluency in speech, for example through repeating sounds or parts of words, whole words or sentences. These children may have a stammer;

• a tendency to mispronounce sounds in words.

In these situations we advise you to discuss any concerns you may have with the Special Educational Needs Co-ordinator. Some children may already have been referred for speech and language therapy and may be receiving targeted intervention. You should already be aware of these children. However, some children may not have been identified and may require targeted intervention. In this case you should speak to the parents about your concerns. The Special Educational Needs Co-ordinator will support you with referrals. Be aware that some children may have been discharged from speech and language therapy support because parents may have missed appointments. In this case you should discuss your concerns with the Special Educational Needs Co-ordinator.

Risks of poor speech, language and communication

The impact of poor speech, language and communication can be significant. These skills are necessary for children to learn effectively throughout the curriculum. Poor achievement in these skills can impact on their achievement and overall life quality. Many children with poor speech, language and communication go on to have reading difficulties, and the gap in reading age tends to widen as children get older. This impacts on children's overall intellectual development because as children get older they need the skill of reading to help them to learn. Children with poor speech, language and communication are at more risk of being bullied. Additionally, lack of achievement can result in these children displaying low self-concepts and social, emotional and behavioural problems. According to the Communication Trust, 60 per cent of people in young offenders institutions have communication difficulties. Early intervention can prevent this downward spiral.

Facilitating talk

One of the most effective ways of facilitating talk in lessons is to extend children's responses by asking them to explain their answers to questions. Conversely, closed questions which require a single response can suppress opportunities for talk and communication. You should plan to ask open questions which enable children to give a range of responses. Giving children time to respond to questions is essential. How many times have you heard teachers suppress a response by jumping in too quickly with an answer before the child has had time to consider the question? How many times have you done this? Planning 'wait time' so that children have time to consider a question is very important. Allowing children time to think in pairs by providing the opportunity to talk through a problem with a partner is also a very common strategy which teachers now use in their lessons. You need to consider how you address incorrect responses from children. A negative response from you could damage their confidence and make them reluctant to speak in the future. Handling these situations with sensitivity is critical.

CREATIVE APPROACH

A range of creative approaches for facilitating language and communication are identified below:

Dialogic teaching

Brien (2012) states that *dialogic teaching involves the development of new understanding together through analyzing, sharing ideas about and reflecting on what is being said* (p 26). This approach can be used to encourage children to share their opinions about texts they have read or heard. The basic premise is that children take ownership of the discussion as they consider specific aspects of the story, including the characters, events, setting and moral. The teacher can initially model the process by taking a greater role in the discussion, but as children become more confident with this approach they should be able to run the discussion with minimal teacher involvement. The approach can be used across the curriculum and does not have to involve a text. For example, children could debate topics of interest or respond to philosophical questions. Children learn to value different opinions within the group and respect each other's contributions.

Drama

Drama is a powerful vehicle for promoting language and communication. Children can use drama to:

- re-enact scenes from stories;
- explore imaginary worlds;
- explore real-life events.

Drama is a cross-curricular tool and can be used in all aspects of the curriculum to enhance children's understanding. Key strategies include:

Paired improvisation

Children can use paired improvisation to solve a particular dilemma from the real world or a dilemma in a story. Two children could take on the role of the wolf in Red Riding Hood and the grandmother. Through conversation the wolf persuades the grandmother to open the door.

Tableaux

In this strategy the children freeze-frame a particular scene, thinking carefully about body language such as facial expressions. The children must create a still image.

Thought-tracking

Once children have created a tableau, you can thought-track them by asking them to say aloud a word, caption or sentence that they are thinking or feeling while they are in the scene. You can touch them gently on the shoulder and ask them to 'come to life' by saying the words.

Hot-seating

Children can pretend to be someone else, such as a character from a story. When they are in the hot seat, other children can hot-seat them to find out more about them. This strategy provides a useful way of encouraging children to ask their own questions, although children will need support with this initially.

Communication across the curriculum

There seems to be a focus on children producing written outputs in many curriculum areas. You need to value children's oral contributions in lessons and view them as outputs in a similar way to the way you view a piece of writing as a valid output. Brien (2012) recommends that one of the best approaches for facilitating discussion is for teachers to stop dominating lessons and to allow children to interact with their peers. This is a very valuable piece of advice. A dominating teacher will inevitably suppress communication. You should provide children with opportunities to engage in paired discussion or group discussion across the whole curriculum, and consequently these speaking and listening opportunities should be identified on your lesson plans.

CASE STUDY

Lucy is a trainee teacher, undertaking her first placement in a Year 2 class. The children are learning about alternative versions of traditional tales. Lucy decides to use the text *The True Story of the Three Little Pigs*. The children enjoy listening to the story, which is written from the wolf's point of view. After reading the story the children are asked to sit in a circle and consider the story. In particular, Lucy asks them to think about whether the wolf is speaking the truth. The children are firstly given thinking time and then time to talk through their ideas with the person sitting next to them. Lucy then runs a whole-class Community of Enquiry where the children listen to different ideas in the circle, build on what other people have said and offer their own responses. Lucy does not dominate the discussion and she lets the discussions evolve, occasionally prompting the children to think about specific points. The children are free to agree or disagree, but know that if they disagree with someone's point of view they must do so respectfully and must explain why they do not share the same opinion.

- What support would children need to reach this level of maturity in their discussions?
- How could you use this approach across the curriculum?

Critical reflection

Some teachers embrace talk and communication in their classrooms. Their classrooms are busy, lively places, and talk is used across the curriculum to promote learning. Other teachers, in contrast, tightly control children's talk. Why do you think this is?

Critical points

This chapter has emphasised the importance of:

» *creating a rich language-enabling environment which provides opportunities for talk and communication;*

» *extending children's language development;*

» *planning opportunities for children to use language and communication across the curriculum;*

» *early identification of children with speech, language and communication difficulties.*

Taking it further

Buckley, B. (2003) *Children's Communication Skills from Birth to Five Years.* Abingdon: Routledge.

3 Auditory and visual discrimination and vocabulary development

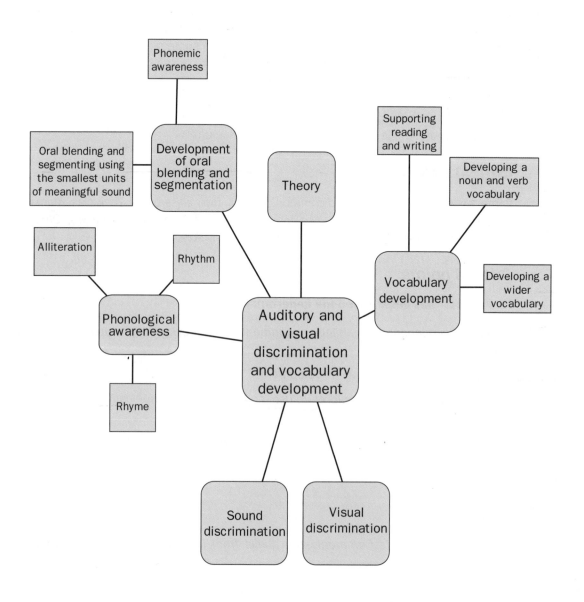

Links to the Early Years Foundation Stage

Communication and language: Listening and attention

Before children can comprehend stories or even begin to learn effectively, practitioners need to develop a range of activities to develop children's skills in listening and attention. This can be done through:

- using visual cues to support what you are saying to children, for example using pictures, objects and gestures and using a talking stick or teddy to facilitate turn-taking;

- using kinaesthetic cues to support what you are saying to children. Activities that involve movement and activity can facilitate experiential learning;

- adapting the language that you use to make it accessible, including limiting the language used so that your explanations are kept simple;

- reducing sensory stimuli such as brightly coloured displays or background noise;

- developing a listening area so that children can listen to rhymes and stories;

- providing opportunities for children to listen to and respond to other children;

- using the child's name to help sustain focused listening.

Without the skill of listening, children do not have secure foundations to begin to learn to read and write. Spending time on developing listening and attention is fundamental to subsequent development in reading and writing.

Communication and language: Understanding

Before children can comprehend text they need to have a good understanding of specific vocabulary including nouns, verbs, adverbs and prepositions. Language development will be addressed in more detail later in the chapter. Children also need to develop an understanding of complex sentences and the meaning of words such as *who/what/where* which frequently appear in children's literature. Without an understanding of language, children's subsequent development in reading will be impeded because language comprehension is a critical skill for effective reading.

Demonstrative nouns

Communication and language: Speaking

As children develop they initially use sounds and then single words to communicate through speech. They subsequently learn to copy familiar expressions and begin to ask simple questions. Children start to use gestures and simple sentences to communicate meaning. Eventually the sentences that they use become more complex as they begin to ask questions and give explanations. Children will develop a breadth of vocabulary based on their experiences. These skills are essential building blocks for their subsequent reading development.

Piaget

Literacy: Reading

The Early Years Foundation Stage (DFE, 2012) focuses on the importance of children's enjoyment of favourite stories, rhymes, songs, poems and jingles. The guidance acknowledges the value of rhyming and rhythmic activities as well as an awareness of alliteration in developing children's early phonological awareness. These are the essential foundations for developing subsequent phonemic awareness.

The theory

Research has found that there is a strong connection between a child's ability to detect rhyme and their subsequent progress in reading and writing (Bryant, MacLean and Bradley, 1990). Tests in rhyme sensitivity and alliteration at the ages of three, four and five predict subsequent progress in reading development over the next three to four years irrespective of intelligence, vocabulary and social background (Bradley and Bryant, 1983, 1985; Bryant, MacLean, Bradley and Crossland, 1990; Ellis and Large, 1987; MacLean, Bryant and Bradley, 1987). Children's early knowledge of rhyme enables them to identify spelling patterns in words that rhyme, and this helps their later development in spelling (Goswami, 1986, 1988). Bradley and Bryant (1983) have identified that training in rhyme has a beneficial effect on reading development, thus suggesting a causal link. Bryant, MacLean and Bradley (1990) have argued that tests in rhyme awareness at the age of four are more significant as indicators of subsequent potential in reading than rhyming tests at the age of six. This is because by the age of six most children will have experience of reading words and will be able to detect rhyming words from similar spelling patterns. Consequently, auditory tests of rhyming ability in the absence of visual representations of print are more reliable indicators of subsequent reading ability.

Literacy development emerges from children's oral language development (Palaiologou, 2010). Throughout this book we adopt an emergent literacy perspective which emphasises a developmental framework for learning to read and write. Children do not suddenly become readers and writers without the pre-requisite skills that lay the foundations for this process. Phonological awareness is part of an emergent literacy framework. This is critical in children becoming formal readers and writers. Sulzby and Teale (1991) describe emergent literacy as 'the earliest phases of literacy development, the period between birth and the time when children read and write conventionally' (p 728). Environmental factors have an impact on children's early literacy development and subsequent abilities in reading and writing. Parents who expose children to rhyme and alliteration and engage children in communication help to develop important precursory skills for literacy. Additionally, rich language and literacy environments in the early years enable children to develop skills in aural and visual discrimination and expose children to print.

Sound discrimination

The ability to distinguish a range of environmental, instrumental, voice and body sounds is critical in supporting children's subsequent development in phonological awareness.

Children need to learn to listen attentively to a range of everyday sounds. They need to be able to describe the sounds they hear and discriminate between them. Children need to be supported to discriminate between loud and quiet sounds; short and long sounds; high and low sounds; fast and slow sounds. They need to be able to describe the sounds they hear, using words including *crashing, banging, stamping, buzzing* and *howling*. Children should be encouraged to imitate sounds that they hear both indoors and outdoors including the sounds of animals, transport and weather. If children are unable to distinguish between everyday sounds they are likely to struggle with distinguishing between language sounds within words and phonemes at a later stage in their development. Teachers need to consider and plan opportunities to develop sound discrimination.

Children can easily be overwhelmed by exposure to too many sounds at any one time. In a busy classroom it can be difficult for children to focus on specific sounds and it is important for activities which focus on sound discrimination that you provide an environment where there are minimal additional auditory distractions.

Musical instruments are a valuable resource for developing skills in sound discrimination. Children initially need to develop an awareness of musical sounds by exploring the contrasting sounds made by different musical instruments. Musical instruments can be played in a range of different ways to create loud and quiet sounds, fast and slow sounds, long and short sounds; and children should be encouraged to identify the differences between musical sounds. You can then give children opportunities to copy a given sound or rhythm using an instrument. It is important that children develop vocabulary to describe the sounds made by different instruments using words such as *soft*, *high*, *low*, *long*, *short*, *loud* and *quiet*. They also need opportunities to identify the source of sounds and to use sounds to represent feelings and movements. You should encourage children to express their feelings and opinions about musical sounds.

Through body percussion, children can begin to develop their awareness of sounds and rhythm. By clapping, patting, tapping, clicking and stamping, children can join in with songs and rhymes, and by listening carefully they should be encouraged to anticipate when to include the sounds. Ask them to perform an action in response to a given sound. For example:

Sound of drum	stamping feet
Maraca	waving hands
Tambourine	tapping fingers

Like in music - Body sounds

Children need to listen carefully for the sounds to perform the corresponding agreed actions. This can be further developed by engaging children in performing a sequence of agreed body actions in response to sound signals.

Children need to produce contrasting body sounds focusing on speed, pitch and rhythm. Their engagement in action songs and rhymes should be encouraged using body percussion. Additionally, children need to learn to keep a steady beat. Get them to copy body sounds and actions and devise some of their own.

Once children become familiar with both instrumental and bodily sounds, you can provide them with opportunities to identify sounds in the absence of visual cues, for example playing a musical instrument or making a body sound behind a screen and asking the child to identify the instrument or body sound and replicate it.

Children need to be able to group instrumental, environmental and body sounds together into categories such as slow and fast, loud and quiet, long and short. The ability to distinguish between everyday sounds and compare sounds will enable children to identify similarities and differences between sounds.

Practising mouth movements (blowing, sucking, tongue stretching) aids articulation. Children need to be given opportunities to explore and generate familiar sounds such as those of running water, a ringing telephone and animal sounds.

Visual discrimination

The skill of visual discrimination is a pre-requisite for learning to read because, in reading, children need to be able to visually discriminate between written representations of the smallest units of sound. These are called graphemes.

Essentially there are two visual skills that children need to develop:

*   a visual memory;
*   visual attention and discrimination.

In developing visual memory, children need to learn to remember visual arrangements. Visual memory can be developed through a range of activities. These include the following.

*   Kim's Game: Show the children a set of three or four objects on a tray and ask them to remember which objects have been shown. Ask the children to close their eyes while you remove one object. Ask the children to open their eyes and identify which object has been removed. This can be extended by introducing more items. The order of the items could be mixed up and the children could be asked to put the items back in the correct order. Alternatively you could ask the children to remember the order of three or four items and the items could be removed completely from the tray. The children could be asked to place the items back on the tray in the correct order.

*   Kim's Game can also be played using photographs, pictures, line drawings and abstract symbols or silhouettes. For example, children could be shown silhouettes of a cat, a dog, a house and a person. One of these could be removed and the children could be asked to identify which silhouette has been removed. In terms of children's development, it is best to start by showing them objects, followed by photographs, pictures and line drawings, before finally showing them silhouettes and abstract symbols.

*   Show the children a teddy dressed in a suit of clothes and ask them to remember the clothes that the teddy is wearing. The teddy can then be placed behind a screen

and an item of clothing taken off. You can then ask the children to identify the missing item of clothing. This activity could be repeated, or extended by putting items of clothing in different positions and asking the children to identify what has changed.

- Show the children a range of three or four shapes and ask them to name the shapes. These can then be placed in the feely bag. In turn the shapes can be removed from the feely bag and the children can be asked to name them. The last shape could be kept in the feely bag and the children can be asked to identify the shape that has been left in the bag.
- Draw a shape using paint or 'gloop' and ask the children to copy it.

You can carry out a range of activities to develop visual discrimination.

- Find the odd one out from a selection of objects where one object is different such as *cat/cat/dog/cat*.
- Find the odd one out from a selection of objects which are the same, for example *lorry/lorry/lorry facing the opposite way/lorry*.
- Find the odd one out where differences are more subtle, for example *boat/boat/ boat/boat with flag/boat*.
- Sort various objects by size, colour and shape.
- Ask children to copy patterns and sequences, for example a string of beads with two or three alternating colours. This can be extended by asking children to copy more complex sequences or to continue a sequence.
- Ask children to point to specific small world items such as a car, a bus, a lorry, a person. This can be extended by asking them to point to a blue car, a red lorry or a yellow bus.
- Spot-the-difference activities require children to identify similarities and differences between two pictures.
- Jigsaws are excellent for developing visual discrimination.
- Perform actions such as tapping shoulders, knees and feet and ask children to copy the action. This can be extended by giving children more complex actions to copy.
- Show children a set of photographs and ask them to identify the odd one out.
- Show children a set of line drawings and ask them to identify the odd one out.
- Show children a set of abstract symbols or silhouettes and ask them to identify the odd one out.

In terms of children's development it is logical to start with object discrimination before moving on to ask children to discriminate between photographs, pictures, drawings, symbols or silhouettes. Children always need to start with concrete experiences, so real objects which they can see and touch are an ideal starting point for developing visual discrimination.

Helps cement the basics then can advance later on

Critical question

» *Visual discrimination is a pre-requisite skill for early reading because children need to be able to distinguish between graphemes. This important skill is not clearly identified within the Early Years Foundation Stage guidance materials (DFE, 2012) as a pre-requisite skill for reading. How will you ensure that you plan to support children's development in this skill?*

Vocabulary development

Children need to understand the meanings of words in order to comprehend what they are reading. You cannot assume that the children in your class will have been exposed to a wide range of vocabulary prior to coming into nursery or pre-school. Some children are raised in language-deprived environments, and conversational interactions with parents and carers may be limited. Additionally, some children may have limited opportunities for language development if parents do not let them experience the wonders of the natural and made world. Taking children out into the immediate locality provides a wealth of opportunities for extending children's understanding of language.

Vocabulary development to support reading and writing

The development of children's understanding of vocabulary such as *beginning, middle, end, before, after* is critical to support children's subsequent reading development. If children do not understand these words they will find it difficult to master the skills of blending and segmentation, because these skills are dependent on children hearing, saying and writing the phonemes they can hear all the way through a word. Thus, teachers will use these words to scaffold children's mastery of blending and segmentation.

Children initially need to understand a variety of everyday vocabulary. They need to be able to understand concept vocabulary such as *round, up, down, over, under, on, small, big, little* so that subsequently they will be able to follow simple instructions for letter formation. You cannot assume that children will automatically understand the meaning of these words. Understanding these words will help children with letter recognition and writing later in their development. Very young children need to explore making dots in the mark-making and creative areas in order to understand the meaning of the word *dot*. Children will be unable to follow instructions to add a dot to letters if they do not understand this word. Children's understanding of *tall* and *short* can be developed through building towers of cubes or bricks or growing plants. These are words which are frequently used when supporting children's transcription skills, so an understanding of these concepts is critical before children start to learn to write. Practitioners need to provide opportunities for children to develop an understanding of concepts such as *big/little/small* through activities such as sorting and matching objects. The concept of a *tail* needs to be understood and children can explore animal tails and pony tails. Children need to explore vocabulary such as *line/ straight* through mark-making and lining up cars in straight lines. Additionally the concept of *halfway* is sometimes difficult for children to grasp and can be developed effectively in the sand and water area by filling containers and buckets. The concept of *cross* can be explored through stories such as *The Three Billy Goats Gruff* as the goats *cross* the bridge. Positional vocabulary such as *above/below/next/between* can be explored through small world activities and in activities where children are required to follow simple instructions to demonstrate their understanding of positional words. Children's understanding of *up/down/ top/bottom* can be explored using stairs and climbing frames, and children can grasp the concept of *round* by engaging in circle games and moving around in a circle.

These are examples of words which children need to understand before they formally start learning to read and write. Children will need to follow instructions when they are learning to read and write, to support their development in blending, segmentation and handwriting. They will be unable to follow an instruction to say the *next* sound in a word if they do not understand the concept of *next*. They will be unable to follow instructions for letter formation if they do not understand words such as *up/down/round/dot/cross*. Time spent laying these foundations for subsequent reading and writing development will be time well spent and you should plan explicit opportunities to teach this vocabulary through adult-led activities. At the same time, opportunities for extending children's understanding of these concepts should be seized during child-initiated and adult-supported learning.

Developing a noun and verb vocabulary

Children need to develop a noun vocabulary. The texts that they will subsequently read will require them to make an association between words and objects. If they are unable to make this association it will be more difficult for them to comprehend the texts that they read. A common way of introducing children to noun vocabulary is to develop their awareness of objects which begin with specific sounds: for example, [o] might be represented by *orange* and [s] might be represented by *snake*. You should take every opportunity to develop children's awareness of noun vocabulary. Children may have been introduced to 'baby-speak' by parents, and therefore children need to be re-taught the correct names for specific objects. Children's awareness of noun vocabulary can be developed in a range of ways, including:

- creating object tables with objects clearly labelled with their names;
- labelling storage areas in the classroom with words and pictures;
- ensuring that you draw children's attention to noun vocabulary during shared reading;
- supporting the sharing of a story with a basket of objects that occur in the story and drawing children's attention to the names of the objects;
- talking to children during child-initiated play. Scaffolding their play in this way provides a valuable opportunity for you to develop children's awareness of noun vocabulary;
- introducing children to common noun vocabulary, such as the names of animals, insects, transport, cutlery, food and other common everyday objects;
- introducing children to the names of body parts.

Children need to be aware that the words they say can be written down. It is therefore important that once children have been introduced to noun vocabulary, they are able to see the written representation of the spoken nouns. They also need to be aware that words that are written down can be read and spoken. Making the link between oral and written language is an essential pre-reading skill and this is why introducing children to objects, pictures, oral and written vocabulary is good practice.

Once children have a good understanding of noun vocabulary it is essential that they begin to develop an understanding of simple verbs. Without a verb vocabulary, children will not gain a complete understanding of the words they subsequently read in texts. Children need to understand the meaning of simple verbs such as *run, walk, jump* and the variations in verb tense such as *walk, walking, walked*. These verbs will appear frequently in the literature that children subsequently read. Following this, children need to be introduced to less familiar verbs including *inflate/deflate/slither*. Again, to support the development of a verb vocabulary, children need to make associations between oral language (spoken verbs), actions and written text. Children need to see verbs written down and they need to be aware that spoken language can be represented as written text and vice versa. *GPC*

In developing children's noun and verb vocabulary, initially the focus is placed on children's oral language development. This can be supported by providing children with a rich language environment which incorporates child-initiated play. Practitioners need to develop a rich language environment by:

- providing children with a range of stimulating activities and resources to explore. Children who are excited will be motivated to use language and ask questions;

- modelling the use of new language regularly. Children need to hear a word several times before they will adopt it in their own language;

- displaying photographs and captions of the children performing actions to support the development of a verb vocabulary, such as *Holly hopping; Jack jumping*. Children are very motivated by seeing pictures of themselves because very young children are egocentric;

- creating curiosity areas in the classroom which stimulate conversation. These areas provide a valuable opportunity to scaffold the development of children's language as well as knowledge and understanding of the world;

- maximising the use of the outdoor environment and educational visits to develop children's noun and verb vocabulary and to develop their knowledge and understanding of the world;

- providing shared reading or communal story-telling opportunities which engage children in performing simple actions to support their understanding of specific noun or verb vocabulary;

- scaffolding children's learning in role-play situations to assist their language development. Practitioners need to provide children with a range of role-play opportunities which relate to both the imaginative world and the real world;

- scaffolding children's language development in sand, water, malleable and construction play;

- playing simple games which focus on the development of a verb vocabulary, such as 'Simon Says';

- providing opportunities for children to recreate stories through drama. Drama provides exciting opportunities for children to use language.

Once children are familiar with oral language (nouns and verbs) they can be introduced to written representations of oral language.

Developing a wider vocabulary

Following the development of a noun and verb vocabulary children need to develop an abstract vocabulary. This includes developing an understanding of adverbs, adjectives and prepositions. Children need to be taught explicitly vocabulary concepts such as *quickly/ slowly/quietly/fast/gently*. Children's understanding of adjectives can be developed by:

- providing children with opportunities to describe a range of everyday materials using words such as *rough/smooth/shiny/dull/soft/hard*;

- providing children with interesting and unusual objects in the curiosity area which they can touch, smell, hear and see. Practitioners can scaffold the children's learning by supporting child-initiated interactions within these areas;

- carrying out tasting activities with food;   *— sensory*
                                                                 activities
- describing the smells of a range of everyday objects;

- providing feely bag activities to enable children to explore objects through touch;

- practitioners modelling the use of descriptive vocabulary in both adult-led and child-initiated activities;

- enhancing sand and water play to include a range of objects for the children to describe, such as textured objects; changing the texture of water to create a thicker consistency; adding colours to water; adding glitter to sand and water; using dry and wet sand; coloured sand;

- providing treasure baskets, with a range of natural materials for young children to feel;

- enhancing malleable play by adding a range of fragrances and textures to play-dough;

- providing a sensory garden in the outdoor area.

Phonological awareness

Phonological awareness is a pre-requisite skill to reading and writing. It relates to a child's ability to distinguish similar and different *language* sounds including tone, tempo, beat, loudness, softness, sound sources (Bruce and Spratt, 2008). It includes awareness of alliteration, rhyme and rhythm. Children with good phonological awareness are well prepared to become successful readers and writers because it provides a basis for developing phonemic awareness, and training in phonological awareness enhances the development of reading in all languages (Goswami and Bryant, 2010).

Rhyme

The importance of immersing very young children in songs and rhymes cannot be overstated. Babies respond to one-to-one interactions as their parents sing to them or recite nursery rhymes. However, teachers and practitioners cannot assume that children will have been exposed to song and rhyme in their home environment prior to starting nursery. Consequently, they should plan regular opportunities for children to participate in these activities in order to facilitate children's phonological awareness. As they develop, it is important that children are encouraged to participate in action songs and rhymes. These could include well-known action rhymes and songs including finger rhymes and counting rhymes. Rhymes which engage the children in anticipating actions are also popular with young children, for example 'This Little Piggy Went to Market'. It is important that teachers and practitioners understand the value and enjoyment that can be derived from songs and rhymes, and opportunities to engage and immerse children in rhyme and song should be identified on a daily basis. Further examples of finger rhymes include:

- 'Incy Wincy Spider';

- 'Here is the Church';

- 'Pat a Cake'.

The next stage of development can also be facilitated through songs and rhymes. They provide a wonderful opportunity to further develop children's understanding of and use of language. This is essential for subsequent reading development. Many songs and rhymes are available in books, and children enjoy interacting with the illustrations. Opportunities should also be planned to engage the children in the development of their gross motor skills as they begin to add large actions to well-known rhymes, for example frogs jumping into a pool ('Five Little Speckled Frogs'). Such activities enhance vocabulary development and focus on the development of listening skills, while at the same time developing gross motor movements.

Many songs and rhymes can engage the children in a range of actions. The song 'Here We Go Round the Mulberry Bush' can be adapted to engage the children in actions to depict washing their hands, cleaning their teeth and combing their hair. Such activities demonstrate the child's ability to understand language. Fine motor skills can also be developed by introducing children to finger rhymes, and such activities will also develop children's understanding of vocabulary.

As children's understanding and use of language develop they will derive great enjoyment from changing the words of familiar songs and rhymes. An example is shown below:

Twinkle, twinkle little car

You go so fast and you go so far.

Children love playing with language and, although initially the adaptations may well need to come from you, it will not be long before they suggest adaptations of their own – the funnier the better. Providing children with opportunities to change the rhyming words in well-known nursery rhymes will strengthen their phonological awareness. The development of fine and gross motor skills should continue to be a key focus as you retell songs and rhymes together.

To further develop children's understanding of rhyme you may wish to consider making the initial changes to a well-known rhyme and then asking the children to complete it. For example, the teacher says:

Humpty Dumpty had a red ball
He threw it over the big brick ... [children predict the word]

There are several well-known rhyming stories that lots of children love, such as *The Gruffalo* by Julia Donaldson, *Hairy Maclary from Donaldson's Dairy* by Lynley Dodd and *Each Peach Pear Plum* by Janet Ahlberg. Children enjoy hearing these stories being retold and, as they are written in rhyme, they quickly recall the words and are soon able to complete rhyming pairs.

A range of additional activities can also be explored to develop children's understanding of rhyme. They will enjoy generating words that rhyme with their own names: *Ben-hen*; *Jack-sack*; *Sam-ham*. Additionally, children enjoy using nonsense words to complete rhyming pairs: *Sophie-bophie* for example. Children can be introduced to rhyming bingo games or games where they are required to identify the odd one out from a set of rhyming objects or pictures.

Immersing children in rhyme should be embedded in daily practice. By hearing rhyme frequently, children have the best possible opportunity to identify it and ultimately generate and use it.

Critical questions

» *How can children's home environment affect their subsequent development in reading?*

» *How can parents and carers support children's understanding of rhyme?*

» *How can schools address the challenge of supporting children whose home environments disadvantage the development of early reading skills?*

Rhythm

The importance of engaging children in activities to hear, copy and create rhythm cannot be overstated. Awareness of rhythm helps children with syllabification as well as developing the skills of blending and segmenting (Bruce and Spratt, 2008). One syllable relates to one beat. Tuning children in to larger sound units within words (syllables) is a pre-requisite for their learning about the smallest units of sound in a word (phonemes).

Rhythm can be introduced through a range of media including songs, music and dance. Young children need to learn to recognise, copy and maintain a steady beat using musical instruments and body percussion. The music selected should have a clear beat, and marching music is a valuable resource for enabling children to respond to a beat. Children should be encouraged to tap, clap, stamp and move their arms to a beat. Additionally, opportunities should be provided to enable them to copy beats and to maintain a chosen rhythm.

Children should be introduced to a range of opportunities to develop their understanding and skills in relation to rhythm. Excited and motivated children will enthusiastically build upon and develop their skills. As a teacher it is your responsibility to create exciting opportunities for children to explore rhythm. Consider carefully the vast range of resources that children naturally wish to explore. These may include sand, pebbles, gravel, combs, brushes, percussion instruments and a range of containers made from different materials. Such resources will enable children to explore the sounds made by different materials for creating rhythms, thus developing the skill of sound discrimination at the same time.

Alliteration

Alliteration supports children in hearing the repetition of one phoneme and initially this focuses the children on a specific sound. Subsequently children's attention should be drawn to the graphemes which represent an identified phoneme. Children enjoy exploring alliterative phrases with their own names, for example:

Jack jumps
Lucy laughs
Sally smiles
Robert runs.

Photographs of the children which match these captions generate great discussion and challenge the children to devise their own alliterative phrases and sentences. These simple phrases can be extended as children develop their understanding of this concept, for example:

Robert runs round Ruby.
Jack jumps on a jet.
Sally smiles and skips.
Lucy laughs loudly.

Critical questions

» *Outcomes for children at the end of the Early Years Foundation Stage are that children should read and understand simple sentences. Additionally children are expected to use phonic knowledge to decode regular words and read them aloud accurately (DFE, 2012, p 29). Reflect on a child that you have worked with who has not achieved these outcomes. What are the reasons for this and are these outcomes possible for all children at this stage of their education? What are the barriers that prevent some children from achieving these outcomes?*

» *The policy focus on teaching children Systematic Synthetic Phonics has become a dominant political discourse in England over the last few years. Consider how the emphasis on teaching children the skills of phonemic awareness can result in the marginalisation of phonological awareness and auditory discrimination.*

» *Consider how the standards agenda in England can result in the marginalisation of phonological awareness and auditory discrimination.*

Development of oral blending and segmentation

In the early stages of blending, children are encouraged to listen to phonemes which they merge in the order in which they are given to identify a target word. Conversely, segmentation develops the skill of breaking down a whole word into its constituent phonemes. Initially there should be a focus on auditory and oral skills to develop children's understanding of blending and segmenting.

During the early stages of phonological development it may be necessary to simplify blending and segmentation through the introduction of compound words. This will enable children to combine two spoken words in a given order to identify a compound word. Examples of compound words could include *snowball, hairbrush or earring*. This will introduce children to early blending skills. Conversely, segmenting can then be addressed by speaking the whole word and challenging the children to identify the two constituent words. The child hears *goldfish* and breaks it down into two words: *gold, fish*.

When children are confidently able to both blend and segment compound words, it is appropriate to develop their understanding of syllables for both oral blending and segmenting. When introducing syllables to children, visual prompts are a very useful resource. We suggest initially presenting the children with three pictures comprising one, two and three syllables respectively, for example *dog, window, computer*. The teacher must slowly articulate and clap each syllable of the word in unison (dog = one clap; win/dow = two claps; com/pu/ter = three claps). The children should be encouraged to orally blend the syllables together to identify the target word. Once the children are familiar with the activity you should encourage them to join you in saying and clapping the syllables of each word. To further develop the skill of oral segmenting, children could be challenged to clap the correct number of syllables and articulate them within a given word. Again, visual prompts are a useful resource for supporting the development of oral blending and segmentation.

Phonemic awareness

Phonemic awareness refers to the skill of hearing and being able to recognise the smallest unit of meaningful sound in words. These are called phonemes. This enables children to develop the necessary skills for oral blending and segmenting. Children achieve fluency in reading faster in languages where there is 1:1 mapping from letter to sound, for example in Finnish and German (Goswami and Bryant, 2010). If there is 1:1 mapping from letter to sound, children are more quickly able to identify phonemes (Goswami and Bryant, 2010). However, where this 1:1 mapping is not evident (for example, in English or French) acquisition of phonemes is slower (Goswami and Bryant, 2010). Additionally, phoneme acquisition is faster in countries that have fewer phonemes – English has approximately 44 phonemes but Finnish has 21 (Goswami and Bryant, 2010) – and is slower in languages that have inconsistent spelling systems.

Oral blending and segmentation using the smallest units of meaningful sound

It is essential that before moving on to the subsequent stage of phonemic awareness, children are confidently orally blending and segmenting compound words as well as syllables. They can now be introduced to orally blending and segmenting consonant–vowel–consonant (CVC) words, including words with vowel digraphs (for example, oa, ea, ee, oi), consonant digraphs (for example, sh/ch/th) and consonant clusters (for example, c-r/b-l/s-p). Children can be challenged to identify the target word as you articulate the phonemes through a word in sequence (oral blending). Additionally, children can then be encouraged to segment a given word into its constituent phonemes through activities such as phoneme counting on their fingers. Again visual prompts are a very supportive resource when introducing this concept. Once children have developed their confidence, the visual prompts should be removed and this will result in a greater reliance on auditory and oral blending and segmenting. It is essential to understand that during the development of oral blending and segmenting, the children should not be introduced to graphemes. The focus is on hearing and orally identifying the sounds within given spoken words (oral segmentation) and merging spoken units of sounds (compound words, syllables, phonemes) together to derive the target word (oral blending).

INTERNATIONAL PERSPECTIVES

The forest schools approach in Scandinavia has been adapted by many schools in other countries including England. This approach maximises the use of the outdoor learning environment for educating children about all aspects of the curriculum.

* Consider how the outdoor learning environment can be utilised for teaching children about aspects of early phonological awareness. Discuss this with your peers and produce a list of ideas.

CREATIVE APPROACH

Mary was a Reception teacher and was keen to develop an enabling learning environment which would support children's development in auditory discrimination and phonological awareness. She had already developed areas of continuous provision inside the classroom to support children's awareness of sound. These included a music area and a listening station with digital recording of environmental sound. Mary was keen to enhance the outdoor provision for developing children's skills in auditory discrimination further.

She introduced a listening tree to the outdoor area. Various everyday objects made from different materials (wood, metal, plastic, etc.) were hung from the tree and children explored the sounds they made. She also introduced a 'talking wall'. Children spoke to each other through a drainpipe which ran across the length of a wall. Differing lengths of metal piping were arranged on a simple frame and the children explored the different sounds these made when tapped by a table tennis bat. Children's voices were digitally recorded in the outdoor area and played back to other children to see if they could identify the voices. The children enjoyed doing this and started to record different voices independently. They played the voices back to other children and asked them to identify the voices.

- Consider other ways in which the outdoor environment could be used to facilitate the development of auditory skills.

- Consider the role of the practitioner in supporting and scaffolding children's independent learning. How can practitioners advance children's learning as they play in the areas of provision?

- How can the outdoor environment be used to support story-telling?

CASE STUDY

Maisy entered her final year in the Early Years Foundation Stage with low levels of attainment in many areas of her development. Social Services and health service practitioners were already involved with Maisy's family, and by working with them the school quickly established a clear picture of Maisy's home life. Her parents were both illiterate and unemployed. There were also two younger siblings. Maisy's father was violent towards her mother and the children. There was little food in the house, the children had a few broken toys and there were no books. The parents regularly sat in front of the television drinking alcohol, smoking cigarettes and drugs. Maisy and her siblings were taken into care during Maisy's final year in the Early Years Foundation Stage.

Maisy's skills in sound discrimination and phonological awareness were under-developed. She struggled to listen attentively for short periods of time and her speech was poor. To support Maisy in her development the practitioners planned a rich programme of opportunities to develop her auditory and oral skills. These included sound walks, rhyming activities, singing familiar songs, listening to stories and making sounds with musical instruments.

Maisy made good progress and by the end of the academic year she was able to read simple sentences and write phonetically plausible words.

- How was Maisy disadvantaged by her home circumstances?

- How can practitioners support parents in developing a language-rich home learning environment?

- What barriers need to be overcome in developing effective partnerships with parents?

Critical reflection

According to Whitehead (1999: 23), it is likely that sensitivity to the rhythms and sound patterns of language is a universal feature of all cultures and their languages, as songs, poems, dances and music from around the world all indicate.

Consider how you can ensure that multicultural opportunities are embedded in your practice to address the learning needs of all children.

Critical points

This chapter has emphasised the importance of:

» *providing children with the pre-requisite skills which lay the foundations for reading readiness;*

» *developing children's skills in phonological awareness, starting with discriminating larger units of sound before introducing children to smaller units of meaningful sounds in words;*

» *a broad and a rich language curriculum within an enabling environment.*

Taking it further

Burnett, A. and Wylie, J. (2002) *Soundaround: Developing Phonological Awareness Skills in the Foundation Stage.* London: David Fulton Publishers.

4 Systematic Synthetic Phonics and how children learn to read

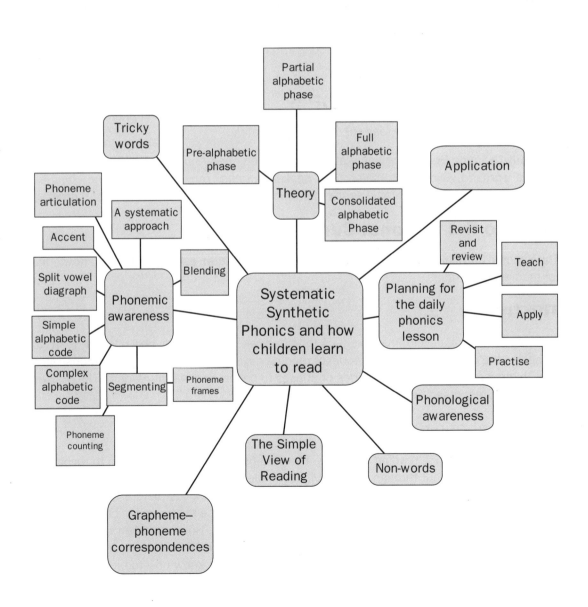

Links to the Early Years Foundation Stage

Communication and language: Listening and attention

The Early Learning Goal for listening and attention states that children need to *listen attentively in a range of situations.*

Communication and language: Understanding

The Early Learning Goal for understanding states that children need to *follow instructions involving several ideas or actions.*

Communication and language: Speaking

The Early Years Foundation Stage emphasises the importance of children building up a bank of vocabulary and using talk to connect ideas and events.

Literacy: Reading

The Early Learning Goal for reading states that children need to use their *phonic knowledge to decode regular words and read them aloud accurately.*

The Early Learning Goal for writing states that children need to *use their phonic knowledge to write words in ways which match their spoken sounds. They also write some common irregular words. They write simple sentences which can be read by themselves and others.*

Links to the National Curriculum

The National Curriculum emphasises the importance of children using their phonic knowledge for reading and writing.

The theory

Theories of reading development help us to understand more clearly how children learn to recognise the printed word. Ehri's model of reading development (Ehri, 1995) demonstrates how children progress through a series of phases to become confident readers. The phases are briefly summarised below:

Pre-alphabetic phase

At this stage, children's 'reading' is largely informed by visual cues. They learn to recognise print in the environment through the use of visual cues including the font style and colours of the text. Many children can recognise the word *McDonald's* well before they can make grapheme–phoneme correspondences. Children will recognise the names of chocolate bars or toys when the words are presented in their usual context. However, when the words are presented in normal text they may struggle to identify the word. Although children at this stage may recognise the sounds of some letters they do not know how to blend sounds to read words. However, children are very aware of environmental print and this demonstrates that they are beginning to understand that print carries meaning.

Partial alphabetic phase

At this stage of their development, children demonstrate the ability to make grapheme–phoneme correspondences and they use this knowledge to read words. However, they do not yet have enough alphabetical knowledge to work all the way through the word. They may read *toy* instead of *tap* and this demonstrates knowledge that the initial phoneme of a word can be used to predict what the word says. However, the over-use of the initial sound as a strategy for reading largely resembles an analytic approach to phonics. As they become more confident and skilled they may focus not only on the beginnings of words but also the endings of words. For example, they may read *shop* instead of *soap*.

Full alphabetic phase

At this stage, children are able to blend the phonemes all the way through the word. When presented with an unfamiliar CVC word, children will be able to read it by saying each phoneme in turn and merging them together to read the target word. Children's ability to blend phonemes in words will be dependent upon the phase of the alphabetic code. Initially children will not be able to blend the phonemes in /b/oa/t/ because they may not have been taught the vowel digraph /oa/. However, after they have been taught this grapheme–phoneme correspondence, they will be able to decode words that may appear to be phonetically irregular. Eventually children will need to rely less on blending as the process of word recognition becomes more automatic. It is a time-limited strategy because children will eventually be able to recognise words through sight.

Consolidated alphabetic phase

At this stage, children begin to recognise a variety of units of sound including phonemes, morphemes, onsets and rimes. For example, children might recognise /str/ in the word *string* and once they learn the rime /ing/ they will be able to instantly recognise words such as *ring*, *king* and *thing*. Children at this stage may not need to read the word by breaking it down into its smallest units of sound (phonemes) and instead they may use the larger sound units within words.

The Simple View of Reading

This conceptual framework developed by Gough and Tunmer (1986) demonstrates how reading is the product of word recognition and language comprehension (see diagram on p 46). Children need both skills to be an effective reader. Children can fall into any of the four quadrants. Effective readers fall in the top right-hand quadrant. Children in the top left-hand quadrant may have an extensive vocabulary and may be able to answer questions about stories they have been told. However, their poor ability to recognise words on a page means that their reading development is stunted and therefore these children require intervention in the area of word recognition. A structured phonics programme which includes the explicit teaching of letter–sound correspondences and how to blend these together to read words is essential for these children. Children in the bottom-right quadrant may be said to be 'barking'

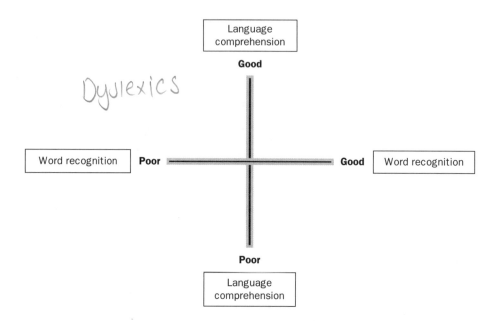

at print. They can read the words on a page but have limited or no understanding of what they read and limited understanding of language. These children require an explicit language development programme which focuses on the structured teaching of language. They also require access to a language-rich learning environment to immerse them in spoken and written language. This will include access to rich play-based learning, drama and role play and speaking and listening activities. Children in the bottom-left quadrant need access to intervention in the area of word recognition and language comprehension.

The model demonstrates to teachers that you need different kinds of teaching to develop children's skills in both word recognition and language comprehension. To develop word recognition you need to teach a structured programme of synthetic phonics as well as introducing children to words which are not phonetically decodable. To develop children's skills in language comprehension you need to plan for the explicit teaching of language by extending children's repertoire of language across the curriculum. The model will be useful as an assessment tool by assessing children's skills in each domain and plotting them on the matrix. The model demonstrates to teachers that you cannot simply assume that a poor reader needs additional phonics intervention. It may be that their skills in word recognition are well developed and that they require access to a language development programme. The nature of the deficit should determine the type of intervention that children require and it is not sufficient to say that a child struggles with reading. The model clearly demonstrates that you need to know why they are struggling and then you can use this information to plan for appropriate intervention.

Critical reflection

The Rose Review (Rose, 2006) recommended that the searchlights model for word recognition be reconstructed into the Simple View of Reading. The National

Literacy Strategy (OFEE, 1998) advocated this framework for teaching reading. The searchlights model as a model for teaching reading focused on teaching children to draw upon one of four cues to read an unknown word. These included:

» *phonic cues: sounding out the phonemes in the word or guessing words from their initial phoneme;*

» *contextual cues: missing out the word and reading ahead to the end of the sentence to get the gist, then going back and making an attempt at the unknown word;*

» *graphical cues: looking at word shape and word length;*

» *grammatical cues: focusing on whether a child's incorrect attempt at an unknown word sounded right and asking the child to adjust their response in the light of this.*

One of the main problems with the searchlights model was that it made phonics an optional strategy for reading unknown words. In the synthetic phonics approach, phonics and specifically decoding all through the word is the prime strategy for reading print. Additionally, the searchlights model led to a great deal of guessing words rather than accurate word identification. The strategies are therefore unreliable and draw heavily on the use of comprehension strategies for word recognition. In reality, word recognition and comprehension are distinct processes which demand different kinds of teaching.

Given that children learn in different ways, do you feel that the decision to abandon the searchlights model was an appropriate decision to make?

Phonological awareness

Phonological awareness is the ability to identify a variety of units of sound within words. This includes awareness of syllables, syllable fragments (onset and rime) and awareness of rhyme. The onset refers to the consonants that come before the vowel, for example /br/ in bring. The rime is the vowel and the rest of the syllable, so in the word *bring* the rime is /ing/. In a synthetic phonics approach we do not teach children to identify onsets and rimes as a reading strategy. To decode *soap* a synthetic approach requires children to identify the phonemes /s/oa/p/ rather than recognising /oap/ as a unit of sound. It is meaningful to hear the smaller sounds represented by the graphemes /s/oa/p/ because these still lead the child to the target word. However, before children start to develop phonemic awareness for reading and spelling, it is useful to get children to hear larger units of sound before focusing on smaller units of sound. From a developmental perspective it is logical for children to divide words into syllables and onsets and rimes before they start to hear the smaller sound units. We support the notion that it is important to teach children about onsets and rimes while they are developing their phonological awareness. This is a stage before children are introduced to graphemes and certainly before we start to ask them to read. The process of developing phonological awareness is largely oral and auditory and is a process which tunes children into sound. If children know that *goat, boat* and *throat* sound the same and if they can hear the units /c/oat/ and put them together to make *coat* then it is an indicator that they have good phonological awareness. Developmentally it is logical for children to hear c/oat/

before they can hear /c/oa/t/ at the oral blending and segmenting stage. It is logical for them to hear the sounds /c/at/ and put them together to make *cat* before they hear /c/a/t/.

Developing children's phonological awareness largely takes place before children are asked to decode words for reading. It focuses on getting children to listen to sounds and putting them together to identify target words. Developing phonological awareness is an auditory and oral process and can be developed using a range of activities. These include:

- asking children to identify the odd one out from a collection of spoken words such as *cat, mat, dog, rat, sat*;

- clapping out the syllables in words such as *al/pha/bet*. All words have at least one syllable and each syllable has one vowel sound;

- singing alliteration songs and making up short alliterative captions;

- sound-talking a word and asking children to guess the word: c/at; p/ig; d/og/; c/oat starting with onsets and rimes before progressing to the smallest units of sound: /c/a/t/; /p/i/g/; d/o/g/ and c/oa/t/.

We do not advocate the teaching of onset and rime once children formally begin to be taught from a structured phonics programme. Once the formal teaching of the alphabetic code begins we believe that the approach should be synthetic and focus on the smallest meaningful units of sound within a word. However, at the early stages of phonological awareness, children need to hear larger sound units in words before they can hear the smaller sound units. Once children are confident with hearing the smallest units of sound and articulating the smallest units of sound, the formal teaching of the alphabetic code can begin, using an entirely synthetic approach.

We strongly advocate that work on developing phonological awareness is an ongoing process which must not stop once children begin to be taught the simple alphabetic code. In the Reception class and Year 1, class teachers should continue to focus on rhyme, alliteration, syllabification and oral blending and segmenting, as well as teaching children how to blend phonemes for reading and how to segment spoken words into graphemes for the purposes of writing. This is an essential part of a broad and rich language curriculum to which all children are entitled.

Oral blending refers to the process of hearing the phonemes within a spoken word and merging them together to identify the target word. An example would be a child hearing /c/oa/t/ and identifying the target word *coat*. Oral segmenting is the ability to separate a spoken word into its constituent phonemes so a child would know that the word *cat* is made up of the phonemes /c/a/t/. Oral blending and segmenting are taught before children are introduced to the graphemes and before they are taught to read and write. It is part of developing children's phonological awareness.

Grapheme–phoneme correspondences

In the English language there are approximately 44 sounds of speech. People vary in terms of how many sounds of speech they say there are. Our language system has developed in complicated ways over time. There are not enough letters of the alphabet to represent all the sounds of our speech because there are only 26 letters. Therefore we need to combine letters into digraphs and trigraphs in order to represent some of the sounds of our speech.

Speech sounds are represented by graphemes. A grapheme is the graphical representation of the phoneme, so the word *float* has four phonemes: /f/l/oa/t/. It also has four graphemes and five letters. There are always the same number of phonemes and graphemes in a word.

When children look at a grapheme and say the corresponding phoneme they are making a grapheme–phoneme correspondence. However, the English language is very complex, and unlike other languages (such as Italian, Spanish or Finnish) the specific speech sounds can be represented by a variety of graphemes. Additionally, a single grapheme can represent several phonemes. As a teacher you need to be aware that graphemes are made up of letters and that a grapheme can be represented by a single letter or a combination of two or more letters. You need to train children in understanding the language of phonemes and graphemes by using simple commands such as '*Look at the grapheme and tell me the phoneme*'. Sometimes trainee teachers and teachers alike are afraid to use what they deem to be complex language with young children. However, children need to be familiar with the terminology of English in much the same way that you would not hesitate to teach them words such as *hexagon* in mathematics or *electricity* in science. The more they hear the words being used the more comfortable they will feel in using them and the more familiar they will become with them.

Phonemic awareness

Phonemic awareness is the ability to hear phonemes within spoken words. A phoneme is the smallest unit of meaningful sound within a word, so in the word *dog* a child is expected to be able to hear the phonemes /d/o/g/. A child with good phonemic awareness is able to hear the phonemes and the order of the phonemes. In the example of *dog*, a child with good phonemic awareness would also know that to change 'dog' into 'fog' the phoneme 'd' would need to be substituted with the phoneme 'f'.

In a Systematic Synthetic Phonics approach, children are taught to hear the smallest units of meaningful sounds in spoken words. Examples are listed below.

Word	Phonemic divisions	Number of phonemes
cat	/c/a/t/	3
moon	/m/oo/n/	3
shop	/sh/o/p/	3
chip	/ch/i/p/	3
snack	/s/n/a/ck/	4
splash	/s/p/l/a/sh/	5
rain	/r/ai/n/	3
drum	/d/r/u/m/	4
goat	/g/oa/t/	3
clap	/c/l/a/p/	4

In the word *moon* it is not meaningful to separate the word into /m/o/o/n/ because it will never sound like the target word. Similarly in *goat* it is not helpful to separate the word into /g/o/a/t/ so it is better to teach /oa/ as a unit of sound. The same applies to *chip* and *shop* where it is not helpful to teach /c/h/ or /s/h/ as discrete sounds within these words. However, in *snack* we do not have to teach the consonant cluster /sn/ because we can hear the phonemes /s/n/a/ck/ all the way through the word. The teaching of consonant clusters such as /bl/, /cr/, /sl/, /sn/, /sm/ and so on represents a form of phonics known as analytic phonics. In the word *snow* we can hear /s/n/ as discrete sounds so it is meaningful to identify these as separate phonemes in the form of /s/n/. We do not need to teach /sn/ as a sound unit. However, in this same word it is not meaningful to identify /o/w/ separately because this will not make it possible to identify the word *snow* and so we teach /ow/ as a unit of sound. So *snow* is broken down into /s/n/ow/. *Stretch* has five phonemes and we can break it down into /s/t/r/e/tch/ so that /tch/ is taught as a unit of sound.

When two letters combine to make one sound we use the term *digraph*. Examples include /ch/, /sh/ or /th/ which are consonant digraphs. We use the term *consonant digraphs* where two consonants represent one sound as in the word /th/e/m/. We use the term vowel digraphs to refer to two vowels which make one phoneme such as /oa/, /ai/ and /ee/ which are examples of vowel digraphs.

When three letters combine to make a sound we use the term *trigraph*. Examples include /igh/ in /l/*igh*/t/ or /tch/ in /s/t/r/e/tch/.

We use the term *adjacent consonants* to refer to the sequence of consonants at the beginning or ends of words. The consonants are positioned next to each other and examples include /c/l/a//p/, /f/l/a/g/ and /b/e/s/t/.

A systematic approach to phonics

The Rose Review (Rose, 2006) emphasised the need for a systematic approach to phonics. Essentially this means that children are taught the phonemes in a clearly defined sequence. Initially children will be introduced to graphemes represented by single letters (for example, /s/ and /c/) before progressing on to consonant and vowel digraphs such as /sh/, /ch/, /ll/, /ff/ and /ae/. Children will subsequently be introduced to trigraphs such as /igh/ air/ and /ear/ and adjacent consonants such as /s/t/e/p/ and /s/p/oi/l/. Once children have been introduced to all the sounds of speech they will be introduced to the spelling variations for all the sounds of speech. For example, the sound /air/ is represented by the grapheme /air/ in *hair* and /ear/ in *bear*. It is also represented by /are/ in *share*. The speech sound /ee/ can be represented by /ee/ in *feet* or /ea/ in *heat*. It can also be represented by /e/ in words such as *me* and *she*. Phonemes can be represented by different spelling variations (graphemes), and the same grapheme can represent different phonemes. Think of the sounds represented by /ch/ in the words *church*, *chemist* and *champagne*. This is called the complex alphabetic code, and the inconsistency of the English alphabetic code is one of the reasons why some children find learning to read and write so difficult. Other languages demonstrate far greater consistency between the sounds of speech and the visual representations of these sounds.

It is logical to teach children a simple code first before progressing on to the complex code. Children need to be taught one spelling variation for each of the sounds of speech. For example, the grapheme /s/ represents a consistent sound in words such as *sun, bus* and *slug*. However, very young children will quickly notice that the alphabetic code is not consistent. A child with the name of Phoebe may know that the initial sound of her name is represented by the grapheme /ph/ rather than /f/. This child is beginning to notice that there are different spelling variations for the sound of speech. For Phoebe it is well worth pointing out that the initial sound of her name is not represented by /f/ but by /ph/ and that the grapheme /ph/ in Phoebe makes the same sound as the grapheme /f/ in the word fat. For this child it is meaningful to make links to the complex code at the same time as teaching the simple code.

Schools need to follow a progression sequence for introducing children to the grapheme–phoneme correspondences. Many schools will choose to follow a commercial synthetic phonics scheme and there are various schemes on the market for schools to choose from. Adhering to one scheme is important because teachers need to follow the sequence for introducing children to the grapheme–phoneme correspondences, starting with a simple code before progressing on to a complex code. Different schemes vary in terms of the exact order in which phonemes are introduced. This is the reason why 'picking and mixing' from different schemes is not advisable, because each scheme will have its own planned progression for introducing children to the alphabetic code. Irrespective of the scheme used, the Department for Education (DFE, 2011), informed by the Rose Review (Rose, 2006), has stated that phonics programmes should enable children to learn specific skills, including:

- grapheme–phoneme correspondences in a clearly defined, incremental sequence;

- how to blend phonemes all through the word in order to read words;

- how to segment words into their constituent phonemes for spelling;

- that blending and segmenting are reversible processes;

- a simple alphabetic code followed by a complex code;

to read and spell high-frequency words, including those that are not phonetically regular.

Phoneme articulation

It is important that children are taught the pure sounds rather than stressing an 'uh' at the end of each phoneme. For example, the letter 's' is represented by the phoneme 'sss' (hissing noise) rather than 'suh'. Enunciating the phonemes correctly is important and all adults who support reading, including parents and carers, need to be familiar with the enunciation of each of the 44 phonemes. It may be worthwhile to run training sessions to help with this. *Letters and Sounds* (DFES, 2007) includes a DVD clip which demonstrates how to articulate the phonemes correctly. As an adult, you will probably need to re-train yourself in the enunciation of the phonemes because incorrect articulation will lead to incorrect spelling.

Accent

As a trainee teacher you might need to be aware of how your own accent may vary from the accent of the children you are teaching. For example, if you are a trainee teacher from south London teaching in the north of England you may pronounce a longer 'a' sound which is typical of southern accents. It is also possible that you may mispronounce 'th' as 'ff'. In these instances it might be necessary for you to modify your pronunication so that the children you are teaching understand you. The aim of teaching English is for children to communicate in standard English, and standard English can be spoken with any accent. However, the problem arises when accent leads to mispronunciation of the phonemes. In this case, the focus is not to change one's accent but to ensure that phonemes are clearly enunciated. The vast majority of phonemes are pronounced consistently across all accents and there may be a need to modify pronunciation of a minority of phonemes so that enunciation is correct. In the case where children need to modify their pronunciation of specific phonemes, they might enjoy speaking like the Queen so that the enunciation is correct. However, this is not the same as speaking posh. Children will need to use standard English later in their lives in a variety of formal situations and therefore it is helpful if children know how to switch accents.

Critical question

» *Should teachers ask children to change their accents in cases where accent leads to mispronunciation of the phonemes?*

The simple alphabetic code

Children firstly need to be introduced to one spelling variation of each of the 44 sounds of speech (phonemes). Different phonics schemes may suggest a different order for teaching the 44 sounds of speech. In phase 2 of *Letters and Sounds* (DFES, 2007) children are introduced to the following graphemes in the order presented below:

s	a	t	p	
i	n	m	d	
g	o	c	k	
ck	e	u	r	
h	b	f, ff	l, ll	ss

The process of blending begins as soon as the children have been introduced to enough graphemes to represent words. Once children have been taught the first six sounds in this table, they can be asked to decode words such as *pat*, *sit*, *pit*, *tip* and *spit*. In synthetic phonics there is no emphasis on rhyme, so children are not taught to read words in families (*cat*, *bat*, *mat*, *sat*, etc.), as this leads to reading by inference rather than blending the phonemes all through the word. The use of word families represents an analytic rather than synthetic approach to phonics. Children are not limited to reading and writing consonant–vowel–consonant (CVC) words at this stage either. *Spit* is an example of a CCVC word. Children are also taught to segment words using the phonemes they have been taught.

In the next stage of *Letters and Sounds* (phase 3), children are introduced to further phonemes including consonant and vowel digraphs as follows:

j	v	w	x
y	z, zz	qu	
ch	sh	th, **th**	ng
ai	ee	igh	oa
oo, **oo**	ar	or	ur
ow	oi	ear	air
ure	er		

There are two phonemes for the grapheme /oo/ (long and short: *moon* and *book*). There are two phonemes for the grapheme /th/ (voiced and unvoiced: *they* and *three*).

At phase 4 of *Letters and Sounds*, children are not introduced to any new grapheme–phoneme correspondences. The focus at this stage is for children to read and spell words containing adjacent consonants such as *desk*, *best*, *shift*, *step* and *spoil*. Again, there is no emphasis on rhyme, so words such as *best*, *nest* and *vest* should not be taught together as this can lead to reading by inference.

The complex alphabetic code

The advanced or complex alphabetic code focuses on introducing children to the multiple spelling variations for each phoneme. Examples are shown in the table.

/ee/	/oe/	/ae/	/oi/	/ue/
ee (keep)	oa (loaf)	ay (say)	oi (oil)	oo (room)
ea (leaf)	ow (show)	ai (rain)	oy (toy)	ue (glue)
e (he)	o (hold)	a-e (cake)		ew (stew)
y (pony)	o-e (phone)	a (table)		u-e (tune)

This table does not represent a complete version of the complex alphabetic code but it does communicate its key principles. It is useful to have a visual representation of the simple and complex code and to study it to develop your own subject knowledge. A visual chart is a really powerful way of becoming familiar with the code. There are various versions of the simple and complex codes. The phonics scheme adopted by your school will be based on a version of the alphabetic code and this is the starting point for you to develop your subject knowledge and upon which to base your planning.

The split vowel digraph

When a vowel digraph is split with a consonant it is called a split vowel digraph. Examples include:

Vowel digraph	Example
ae	Cake
ie	Like
oe	Pole
ee	Pete

Children need to be able to recognise the digraph as a phoneme so when blending the phonemes in the word *cake* they pronounce the phoneme for /c/ followed by the phoneme for /ae/ followed by the phoneme for /k/. Children used to be taught about magic 'e' changing the vowel sound from its sound into its name, but this teaches children various misconceptions and should be avoided. Magic 'e' is not part of a synthetic phonics approach and neither are silent letters.

Blending

Blending (or decoding) refers to the ability to identify the phonemes (sounds) made by the graphemes all the way through a word, and the ability to combine these in order to read the target word. Blending is for reading. Thus, children look at the word *coat* and say the phonemes represented by the graphemes /c/oa/t/ in order to read the target word. In synthetic phonics, blending is the prime strategy through which words are read. It is a time-limited strategy which develops the skill of quick and accurate word recognition. When modelling this skill you need to point to the graphemes in turn through a word and encourage the children to say each phoneme. Initially you will need to point to the graphemes slowly, and in turn the children are encouraged to say the corresponding phonemes. You can then push the graphemes closer together or point to them faster to enable the children to make more automatic links between the phonemes and the target word.

The Simple View of Reading demonstrates that the skill of word recognition is one of the fundamental skills associated with being a good reader, and without the skill of word recognition children will certainly not have any understanding of what they are reading. However, in the initial stages where the emphasis is on decoding, there will be less emphasis on developing children's comprehension. Once children are fluent decoders you will be able to concentrate on developing their reading comprehension skills. In the early stages while children are concentrating on decoding you can aid their understanding of the texts they read by talking to them about the story, its events and characters and you can ask them simple questions about the text. Fundamental skills include being able to retell simple stories, make predictions and talk about characters. You can help children to understand the stories they read by talking about them as they read and by using simple questions such as *What do you think will happen next?* You should not ignore comprehension while children are decoding, but greater emphasis should be placed on decoding. Once decoding and fluency are mastered by children, you can give greater focus to developing their comprehension skills as children move from learning to read to reading to learn.

When you teach blending you might find it useful to use sound buttons so that children can identify the phonemic divisions within words. Examples include:

bat

chip

These marks clearly help children to identify the phonemic divisions within words and to identify the digraphs and trigraphs.

Segmenting

Segmentation is the reverse of blending. It is the ability to split up a spoken word into phonemes and to select the graphemes to represent those phonemes. Segmentation is for spelling. Firstly children practise the skill of oral segmentation. When given the word *mat* they need to be able to identify the constituent phonemes /m/a/t/ all the way through the word by saying the corresponding phonemes. A progression from this is for children to be able to select magnetic letters or letter cards to represent a spoken word or picture. When shown a picture of a rat the children should be able to select the corresponding graphemes /r/a/t/ to build the word. This early word-building is essential for all children but particularly for children who have poor motor control and may find it difficult to write down the corresponding graphemes. Ultimately children need to use the skill of segmenting as a spelling strategy. When faced with a word that they are not sure how to spell, children should be encouraged to write down the graphemes for the phonemes they can hear all through the word in the correct sequence. While children are developing their confidence as writers in the early stages of writing, the focus should not be on producing correct spellings but simply on making a phonetically plausible attempt. In order to support children in writing the graphemes corresponding to the phonemes, it is useful if they have a simple alphabet mat or chart in front of them to help them select the correct graphemes.

Phoneme frames

A phoneme frame is a useful resource to provide children with when you are teaching the skill of segmenting. Each grapheme is written into a box and examples include:

a	t

f	o	g

f	l	a	g

s	p	l	a	sh

s	t	r	e	tch

r	oa	d

Phoneme counting

When teaching children to segment words into their constituent phonemes and graphemes, a useful strategy is to say the word and to ask the children to count the number of phonemes they can hear using their fingers. This will help them to decide which graphemes to select to represent the written word. Variations of this include tapping out the phonemes by tapping knees or gently patting the head. Additionally, children can walk the word, so for the word *pin* they would walk three strides as they say the word /p/i/n/.

Non-words

In 2012 the government introduced a reading test, which includes non-words, to all children in Year 1. Children are presented with a range of decodable non-words which they have never seen before. The only way they can work out what the word says is by sounding out the phonemes and blending them together to read the words. The test is designed to assess children's ability to decode words using blending as the prime approach. The reading test is not designed to assess children's language comprehension skills. Given the political focus that this test has and the need for schools to demonstrate that they are teaching children to decode using blending as the prime approach, it is essential that you ask children to read both decodable words which are real and those which are made up. Children can be asked to sort real words from those that are nonsense words.

Critical questions

» *Is the non-word reading test an effective measure of children's reading skills?*

» *What are the arguments for and against this test?*

Tricky words

Tricky words are those which are not phonetically decodable all the way through the word. Take the word *said* as an example. It will not be beneficial for a child to sound out /s/a/i/d/

because saying these graphemes in isolation will not help children to say the target word. In order to teach tricky words you first need to point out the part of the word that is regular. In the example of *said*, the tricky part of the word is represented by *ai*, and in this word these two letters make the sound 'e'. If you make this teaching point, it is then possible to approach the word in a partially phonetic way because the initial and final letters are phonetically regular. When segmenting the word, the children can write the first grapheme because it is phonetically regular. They can then write the tricky part of the word followed by the final grapheme which is phonetically regular.

High-frequency words are commonly occurring words, and children's reading and writing development will be impeded if they do not quickly learn to read and spell these words. Some high-frequency words are phonetically decodable. These include words such as *help*, *mum*, *dad*, *can* and *from*. Word lists of the most common 100 words can be readily located. However, many of the high-frequency words are tricky words which cannot be decoded using the simple alphabetic code, although it may be possible to decode them once children are familiar with the complex code.

Tricky words can of course be learned as whole units, for example using a traditional 'look, say and remember' approach. However, this approach only tends to be successful for children with good visual memories. Children are likely to need to see a word several times before they remember it, so drawing children's attention to the parts of the word that are phonetically irregular provides them with a strategy for working out how to read and write the word.

The use of mnemonics may aid children with spelling tricky words. This is a strategy whereby children are taught to remember a caption to aid the process of spelling the word, for example, Sally-Anne is dancing = *said*.

Critical questions

»   *High-frequency words include tricky words and decodable words. Taking this into account, do you think that all the high-frequency words should be displayed in the classroom on the word wall as an aid to spelling?*

»   *What are your views on teaching children to read tricky words through a whole-word approach?*

Application

Children need opportunities to apply the skills they learn in taught phonics sessions into their general reading and writing. School inspectors now focus heavily on the quality of teaching in synthetic phonics. This will partly be evaluated through observation of synthetic phonics lessons but also through inspectors listening to children read. Inspectors will need to be satisfied that children are able to use blending as the prime approach to decoding when they are faced with a word they do not know how to read. Synthetic phonics can only be good or outstanding if it gets children reading and writing. When you work with children on an individual basis in reading, it is important that you focus on the development of children's decoding skills on a one-to-one basis. This can also be reinforced in guided reading and shared reading sessions with the whole class. Similarly, during guided and independent writing, children need to be encouraged to make phonetically plausible attempts at unknown spellings and this will be evident through looking at samples of children's writing. For children in the early years it is more important that they demonstrate the skills to write independently than be able to produce work that is all spelt correctly. Children's writing should demonstrate that they are making attempts at segmenting words into their constituent phonemes, rather than the spelling being perfect. In fact, perfect spelling may lead inspectors to assume that the words have been given to the pupils and that they have simply copied them down, thus demonstrating lack of independence on the children's part. Phonetically plausible attempts at spellings enable teachers to pinpoint clearly children's development in writing. Focused, diagnostic marking will, over a period of time, enable children to become better spellers, but children need to have sufficient skills to make phonetically plausible attempts at reading and writing to give them the confidence to read and write independently.

Critical question

»   *What are the arguments for and against children making phonetically plausible attempts at spelling?*

Planning for the daily phonics lesson

The Rose Review (Rose, 2006) recommended short, discrete, daily sessions of phonics securely embedded within a broad and rich language curriculum. The best phonics teaching takes place at a brisk pace and engages children in rich, multi-sensory activities so that new phonic knowledge is embedded through children's visual, auditory and kinaesthetic channels.

Letters and Sounds (DFES, 2007) recommended a four-part structure to the daily phonics session. The lesson is structured using the following elements:

Revisit and review

In this stage in the lesson, previously taught grapheme–phoneme correspondences are revisited, particularly those that pupils have found difficult. You can also revisit tricky words that have previously been taught. In addition, you may decide to revisit the skills of blending and segmenting by providing children with words that are within the children's existing phonic knowledge.

Teach

In this part of the lesson you will introduce children to new learning. You might teach them a new grapheme–phoneme correspondence and/or a new tricky word.

Practise

In this part of the lesson you will ask the children to practise blending and segmenting words which incorporate the newly taught grapheme–phoneme correspondence. It is important to present the children only with words that are within the level of the alphabetic code which they have been taught. There is very little point in presenting children with words that are beyond the level of their existing phonic knowledge. You might also focus on asking the children to write the new tricky word.

Apply

In the final part of the lesson you should present the children with a caption or a sentence. This should be within their existing phonic knowledge and it should incorporate words which include the newly taught grapheme–phoneme correspondence. It should also include tricky words which have previously been taught and any new tricky words which have been introduced in the lesson. For children in the Early Years Foundation Stage you might also place the newly taught grapheme–phoneme correspondence into areas of continuous provision. Hiding graphemes or tricky words in the sand or placing them in the writing area provides opportunities for children to practise writing them. Additionally, providing children with opportunities to blend phonemes for reading and to segment words into their constituent phonemes for spelling in the continuous provision provides children with valuable opportunities to consolidate their newly acquired phonic knowledge.

The current Ofsted inspection framework for schools (Ofsted, 2012) places less emphasis on teachers following a particular model of teaching. You now have more freedom to structure lessons in ways that you feel are appropriate as long as it is evident throughout the lesson that children are learning and making progress. However, we do recognise that as a trainee teacher you might find this four-part structure helpful in developing your confidence in teaching phonics. Once you become confident you can deviate from this prescribed approach.

CREATIVE APPROACH

Observations of phonics lessons had identified that the majority of teachers were heavily reliant on the use of individual whiteboards and pens for children to show their responses to questions. The school wished to further develop practices which engaged the children in active learning but with a variety of approaches. This was communicated to staff but the response was slow. Consequently a training event was planned and four open-ended activities were introduced to all staff. Working in pairs the staff then planned an open-ended activity of their own. Each pair shared their ideas, resulting in staff leaving the training event with a bank of useful approaches to support their own teaching.

CASE STUDY

Leon was a confident trainee teacher working in a Reception class. He quickly identified the need to support parents to articulate phonemes correctly and to also develop their understanding of blending and segmenting as well as the teaching of tricky words. He discussed this with his mentors and together they planned and delivered a workshop for parents to address the issues that had been identified.

Critical reflection

There are many children in Key Stage 2 who struggle to read. These children have been taught through a synthetic phonics approach. The Ofsted inspection framework (Ofsted, 2012) asks inspectors to examine strategies used to support

these children, and schools are expected to demonstrate the systematic teaching of synthetic phonics in Key Stage 2 for children who are not reading.

»   *Given that these children have already been taught a synthetic phonics approach do you think it is appropriate that the same approach is being recommended for these children in Key Stage 2?*

»   *Does one approach to reading meet the needs of all children?*

Additionally, the synthetic phonics approach focuses on blending as the prime strategy for word recognition. Analytic approaches use a mixture of strategies including guessing words from the initial phoneme, and the explicit teaching of onsets and rimes through presenting children with words that have different onsets but the same rhyming strings.

»   *Given that it may be more efficient for children to recognise larger sound units (rimes and consonant clusters), do you agree that children should be taught using a synthetic approach which requires children to identify the smallest units of meaningful sounds within words?*

»   *What are the benefits and limitations of children learning to read using larger sound units?*

Critical points

This chapter has emphasised:

»   *the importance of developing your own subject knowledge in relation to the simple and complex alphabetic codes;*

»   *the meaning of specific vocabulary including phoneme, grapheme, blending, segmenting, digraphs and adjacent consonants;*

»   *the need to articulate phonemes correctly;*

»   *the value of the Simple View of Reading as a conceptual framework upon which to base the teaching of reading.*

Taking it further

Johnson, R. and Watson, J. (2007) *Teaching Synthetic Phonics.* Exeter: Learning Matters. This book provides a comprehensive overview of reading development and each of the phonic phases in *Letters and Sounds*.

Lewis, M. and Ellis, S. (eds) (2006) *Phonics, Practice, Research and Policy.* London: Paul Chapman.

Togerson, C.J., Brooks, G. and Hall, J. (2006) *A Systematic Review of the Research Literature on the Use of Phonics in the Teaching of Reading and Spelling.* London: DFES.

5 Creative approaches for teaching Systematic Synthetic Phonics

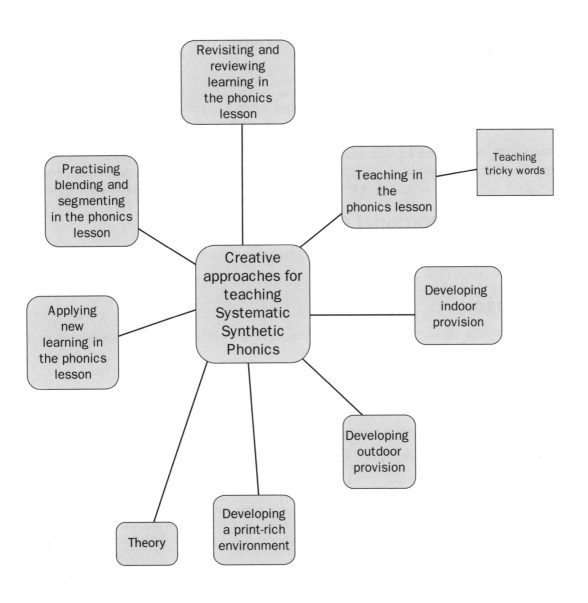

Links to the Early Years Foundation Stage

Communication and language: Listening and attention

The Early Learning Goal for listening and attention states that children need to *listen attentively in a range of situations*.

Communication and language: Understanding

The Early Learning Goal for understanding states that children need to *follow instructions involving several ideas or actions*.

Communication and language: Speaking

The Early Years Foundation Stage emphasises the importance of children building up a bank of vocabulary and using talk to connect ideas and events.

Literacy: Reading

The Early Learning Goal for reading states that children need to use their *phonic knowledge to decode regular words and read them aloud accurately*.

The Early Learning Goal for writing states that children need to *use their phonic knowledge to write words in ways which match their spoken sounds. They also write some common irregular words. They write simple sentences which can be read by themselves and others.*

Links to the National Curriculum

The National Curriculum emphasises the importance of children using their phonic knowledge for reading and writing.

The theory

The Rose Review (Rose, 2006) emphasises the importance of using a multi-sensory approach for the teaching of phonics. This includes:

* visual auditory and kinaesthetic activities;

* physical movement to copy letter shapes;

* the use of magnetic letters for word building;

* the use of picture cues and actions to accompany phonemes.

According to the Rose Review:

Multi-sensory activities featured strongly in high quality phonic work and often encompassed, variously, simultaneous visual, auditory and kinaesthetic activities involving, for example, physical movement to copy letter shapes and sounds, and manipulate magnetic or other solid letters to build words.

(2006, para 57, p 21)

Although learning style theory has been rejected by some, we support the premise that children learn more effectively if the learning takes place through a combination of their visual, auditory and kinaesthetic channels. We do not support the notion of grouping children into specific styles of learner. Effective teachers use a combination of approaches to enable all children to access the learning.

Critical questions

The Rose Review emphasises that children often draw on all sensory pathways when they are learning rather than limit themselves to one sensory channel. This raises critical questions around learning style theory, which has tended to assume that children can be categorised by their preference for one particular learning style, ie auditory, visual or kinaesthetic.

»   *Read some critiques of learning style theory. The work of Frank Coffield will be useful in this respect.*

»   *Do you think that learning style theory is helpful?*

»   *What are the advantages and disadvantages of using learning style theory?*

»   *Why is a multi-sensory approach important, ie encouraging children to draw on all sensory channels?*

Revisiting and reviewing learning in the phonics lesson

Every phonics lesson should begin with a short and focused opportunity for children to revisit and consolidate prior learning. This part of the lesson can serve a range of purposes but you should always consider the need for a clear focus. Possible foci could include:

* consolidating previously taught phoneme–grapheme or grapheme–phoneme correspondences;

* listening to previously taught phonemes which are articulated in sequence, blending these together to identify the target word (oral blending);

* identifying, within written words, the phonemes represented by the graphemes and blending these to read a word, caption or sentence within the children's existing phonic knowledge (blending);

* hearing and saying phonemes in spoken words within children's existing phonic knowledge (oral segmentation);

* hearing the phonemes in words within the children's existing phonic knowledge and visually representing the corresponding graphemes through the word to spell the target word(s) (segmentation);

* identifying previously taught tricky words and drawing attention to the tricky part and any phonetically plausible part(s) of a word.

The teaching of synthetic phonics is heavily reliant upon rigorous, frequent and accurate formative assessment. Revisiting prior learning in every lesson must be planned with a clear purpose in mind. It is only through clear identification of individual and group needs that revisiting prior learning can impact positively on achievement. The effective teaching of synthetic phonics necessitates a systematic approach where there is a clear teaching sequence to enable children to build on their prior learning. However, you must always consider that teaching does not necessarily equate to learning. All children will not automatically acquire knowledge, skills and understanding at exactly the same time. You must value and implement strategies to effectively support the assessment of individuals and groups of learners. Assessment is critical to identifying the learning needs of all children. You should use your ongoing assessments to identify the focus for this part of the lesson. An illustration of this point is that children may be able to identify a trigraph, when it is presented to them in isolation, as a grapheme and may quickly articulate the corresponding phoneme. However, when the trigraph is presented within the context of a word some children may have difficulty identifying the phoneme. For example, children may easily articulate the corresponding phoneme when presented with the trigraph /igh/. However, they may then struggle to identify this same trigraph within the word f/l/*igh*/t. This difficulty in transferring learning should be identified through your assessments and addressed by revisiting it at the beginning of subsequent lessons. Additionally, some grapheme–phoneme correspondences do not immediately become automatic for children and these should also be revisited, as should tricky words which may also be problematic.

Throughout the lesson you should aim to maximise the participation of all children. This is also pertinent when you revisit prior learning. You must develop strategies to facilitate children's engagement and participation in all aspects of the lesson. You should avoid:

- a 'hands-up' approach which gives permission for children to disengage from the learning;

- activities which require children to wait their turn, resulting in wasted learning time for the majority of the group or class;

- repetitive and predictable activities which may lead to children lacking motivation;

- passive learning which is dominated by teacher voice and over-focuses on auditory learning;

- allowing over-confident children to dominate the lesson.

If you choose to adopt a 'hands-up' approach then this will only enable one child to demonstrate their knowledge, skills and understanding. Children can also choose not to respond. You cannot assume that a raised hand will automatically result in a correct response. The only child who can effectively be assessed by using this strategy is the child who is chosen to respond. Turn-taking slows down the pace of a lesson and can result in some children becoming disengaged. Additionally, it is too easy to over-rely on a limited range of teaching strategies. A common example of this is the use of mini-whiteboards and pens for 'show me' activities. These are activities which engage all children in writing on a whiteboard and showing their responses to the teacher. While this activity does facilitate children's participation in learning and is easy to resource, its predictability can result in lessons that lack excitement and some children can quickly lose motivation. Lessons which are dominated by the teacher's voice only require children to appear to be listening. Within these lessons there are few opportunities for assessing achievements and learning needs, and passive children can quickly lose interest. In all classes you will encounter some very confident children. However, you must develop inclusive teaching strategies which communicate the expectation that all children will consistently respond to your questions and instructions.

To facilitate children's participation in learning, you should consider:

- approaches which enable all children to actively respond to teacher instructions and questions together;

- the percentage of time given to children waiting for their turn;

- varying the teaching strategies used so that children remain excited and motivated to learn;

- using a range of visual, auditory and kinaesthetic approaches to learning and teaching and varying the activities used within lessons;

- maximising children's engagement by providing them with opportunities to respond actively throughout the lesson;

- cultivating a climate in which there is an expectation that all children will respond to teacher instructions and questions.

CREATIVE APPROACH

When you plan to revisit prior learning, the activities should result in the full participation of all children. In the outdoor area or hall, randomly display multiple copies of six previously taught graphemes which require further consolidation. Initially, revisit each grapheme–phoneme correspondence with the children. The subsequent activity should be brisk as you articulate the phonemes in turn and all children respond by running and standing next to the appropriate grapheme. Observation of the children's responses serves as a valuable assessment strategy.

- What are the benefits of this approach to learning?

- Children who lack confidence may be observed simply following the lead of their peers. Can you identify the advantages and disadvantages of this occurrence?

- How could this activity be adapted to revisit other foci for learning in this part of the lesson?

Using small buckets of water and a broad paintbrush, all children can consolidate their understanding of phoneme–grapheme correspondence. Initially identify two or three graphemes which require further consolidation with a small group of children. Ask the children to articulate each phoneme in response to a shown grapheme. You then articulate each phoneme in turn, and the children all respond by writing the corresponding grapheme using their paintbrushes and water on walls, the floor, coloured sugar paper or chalk boards.

- How does this activity support you in making individual assessments of each child and planning for future learning?

- Consider other ways in which prior learning can be revisited in the outdoor area.

Another useful activity for revisiting prior learning is to seat the children in a circle and give every child a card with a previously taught grapheme. You will need multiple copies of graphemes so that several children have the same grapheme. You start the game by shouting out a phoneme, and children holding the corresponding grapheme are required to stand up and swap places. You can then continue the game by choosing a different phoneme to shout out. This game maximises pupil participation because the children are actively engaged in the activity and several children are required to participate in response to each prompt from the teacher.

You need to develop a bank of activities for revisiting prior learning. This will help to maintain children's interest because over-reliance on any one activity could result in children becoming disengaged. It is important to be mindful that revisiting prior learning should only constitute a few minutes at the beginning of the lesson. For this reason you should always ensure that the activities are focused and brisk.

Teaching in the phonics lesson

This part of a lesson should be dedicated to the introduction of very focused and new learning. This could include:

- opportunities to engage the children in the auditory discrimination of a new phoneme;

- introducing children to a new grapheme–phoneme correspondence;

- teaching children a new tricky word.

You must ensure that planning takes careful account of systematic progression in children's phonic knowledge. You should follow a teaching sequence from the synthetic phonics scheme adopted by your school. There are a range of commercial schemes available for teaching synthetic phonics, and they all differ slightly from each other. In your placement school, ensure that you familiarise yourself with the scheme that has been adopted. Refer to the Teachers' Guide that supports the scheme as this will enable you to understand the progressive sequence of teaching to which you must adhere. Find out about the idiosyncratic features of the scheme you will be using and the principles upon which it is based. Additionally, assessments of individual children's phonic knowledge and skills will enable you to identify prior learning as well as 'next steps' for groups and individuals, and these will support you with the planning process.

It is essential to carefully consider a multi-sensory approach to teaching. Phonics lessons should be taught on a daily basis and children must find them stimulating. An over-reliance on one approach to introducing new learning will cause children to disengage. Frequently teachers rely too heavily on one approach for introducing new phonemes, graphemes or tricky words. Often lessons quickly become predictable as teachers over-use the strategy of modelling on a whiteboard and ask children to identify the phoneme, grapheme or tricky word.

CREATIVE APPROACH

It is important that you actively engage all children throughout this part of the lesson. New grapheme–phoneme correspondences should be introduced to children through all their sensory channels. Children need to see the grapheme and hear its corresponding phoneme, and need opportunities to transcribe the grapheme. Teaching is more effective when children have opportunities to access learning through their visual, auditory and kinaesthetic channels at the same time. Learning is deeply embedded when children can hear and say the phoneme at the same time as seeing and writing the grapheme.

You should introduce all new graphemes, phonemes and tricky words through clear modelling. Children need to be shown the grapheme and introduced to the corresponding phoneme. Children learn more effectively when the new grapheme is clearly transcribed by you. This enables them to see the correct formation and sequence of letters. Children then need to be provided with opportunities to repeat the phoneme and transcribe the grapheme in unison. You need to use a range of well-considered resources and teaching strategies to support the transcription process. These could include:

- air writing or tracing graphemes on the floor;
- tracing graphemes on a partner's back;
- tracing graphemes on the palm of their hand;
- tracing graphemes in sand, salt or glitter trays;
- tracing graphemes in dry compost.

This part of the lesson can be taught in different areas of the school. Examples could include:

- teaching on the carpet area;
- teaching in the outdoor area;
- teaching in the hall;
- working on tables.

You need to consider the impact of using the same location every day to deliver phonics teaching. Effective teachers offer children variety in terms of resources, activities and location. Once children are familiar with the range of media, you may wish to encourage them to make their own choices about which medium to use.

Teaching tricky words

Tricky words are words that are not phonetically plausible. Examples include *he, she, the, said, come*. To teach these effectively it is often useful to initially allow the children to read the words independently. They will usually adopt a phonic approach to doing so. You must not devalue such attempts. Indeed, you should confirm that they have blended phonemes effectively but that the word is 'tricky'. The most effective way of teaching tricky words is to initially identify the regular parts of the word. For example, the 's' and 'd' in the word *said* are regular and these should be identified. You then move on to identify the irregular part of the word (ai) and emphasise it by circling or underlining it and articulating the sound it makes (e). Alternatively, introduce the word and ask the children to write *said* on a mini whiteboard. Most children will write s-e-d. Again, it is important that you acknowledge their attempts before explaining that it is a tricky word. Acknowledge the accuracy of the initial and final sounds (s/d) before drawing the children's attention to the tricky bit in the middle of the word.

Practising blending and segmenting in the phonics lesson

One you have introduced a new grapheme–phoneme correspondence this becomes the key focus of the lesson. Once the children can recognise the grapheme and say its corresponding phoneme, you then provide them with opportunities to:

- read words which incorporate the newly taught phoneme (blending);
- write words which incorporate the newly taught grapheme (segmentation).

In many of the lessons we have observed, trainee teachers have tended to over-emphasise blending at the expense of segmenting. You will need to use your own professional judgement to achieve a balance between engaging children in opportunities for blending and segmenting. Both aspects can be addressed within the same lesson although there may be time constraints if the daily lesson is short.

In synthetic phonics there is no emphasis on onset and rime. The newly taught grapheme/phoneme should therefore be presented to children in different positions within words. For example, when introducing the grapheme 'ea' you could present the children with words such as *eat, meal* and *tea* rather than presenting them with *meat, heat* and *beat*.

All words presented to children in this part of the lesson should be derived from their existing phonic knowledge. You will know which phonemes and graphemes the children have already been taught. You therefore need to identify words for blending and segmenting using only the previously taught phonemes and graphemes and the new grapheme–phoneme correspondence that children have been introduced to in the lesson. For example, if the children have only previously been introduced to the grapheme–phoneme correspondences *s, a, t, p, i* and the new grapheme–phoneme correspondence is *n* then the children could be given words such as *nap, ant, span, spin, snap, pant* and *pin* to blend and segment but they should not be given words such as *and*, *nut* and *can* because the phonemes *d*, *u* and *c* respectively have not been taught.

When you present children with words to blend and segment it is important that you also introduce children to non-words. These are words that are not part of the English vocabulary. If the children have only previously been introduced to the grapheme–phoneme correspondences *s, a, t, p, i* and the new grapheme–phoneme correspondence is *n* you could present them with words such as *ans, nis, san, sant, nisp* and *ansi*. Presenting children with these unfamiliar words is a valuable assessment strategy which enables you to effectively assess their ability to both blend and segment. Children will not be able to rely on memory to read or write these words and instead they will have to use their phonic knowledge.

In 2012 the government in England introduced a phonics screening assessment for all children at the end of Year 1. This assessment includes non-words. Children who are unfamiliar with non-words could be disadvantaged in this assessment and therefore children need to be provided with opportunities to blend and segment both real words and non-words which are within the scope of their existing phonic knowledge. Additionally, children should be given opportunities to sort real words and non-words into these two categories. The following case studies exemplify some of the issues that we have encountered following the implementation of the non-word reading assessment.

CASE STUDY

The cohort of children that we assessed in the Year 1 phonics screening test had exited the Early Years Foundation Stage the previous year. Analysis of the summative assessment data from the Early Years Foundation Stage indicated that 83 per cent of this cohort were achieving national expectations or above in their ability to apply their phonic knowledge to reading. However, when the same cohort was presented with the phonics screening test 12 months later, only 13 per cent passed the test. Many of the children had become fluent readers with good early comprehension skills. This was supported and evidenced by assessment systems in the school. While administering the phonics screening test, teachers noted that many children were able to orally blend the phonemes but their final response for the target word was incorrect. This was because they changed the non-word to the nearest familiar real word which they offered as their answer.

Critical questions

»   *What skills does the phonics screening test assess?*

»   *Drawing on the Simple View of Reading, what skills does the phonics screening test not assess?*

»   *Do you think the phonics screening test is a useful assessment tool for teachers?*

»   *In what ways might this test be detrimental to young readers?*

>> *In what ways might the test lead to labelling young children?*

>> *In what ways might the test be used as a tool for monitoring teacher or school effectiveness?*

CASE STUDY

The phonics screening test was administered to all Year 1 children. This included one non-English speaking child who had arrived from Poland ten weeks prior to the test. At the time of the test he communicated using some single words and gestures and had been included in Systematic Synthetic Phonics lessons alongside his peers from the point of his arrival. He had received no additional phonics input prior to the test. During this time he had developed the skills of identifying some simple phonemes and he was using these to read and write isolated words within his phonic knowledge. Although he did not pass the test, his score was significantly higher than that of 40 per cent of other children.

Critical questions

>> *Why do you think that some of his peers were less successful in the phonics screening test than he was?*

>> *His score was significantly higher than that of the majority of his peers but does this make him a more effective reader?*

CREATIVE APPROACH

As part of a topic on 'space' in a Reception class, an interactive display was created to engage the children in both reading and writing non-words. Each day speech bubbles communicated messages from aliens to the children. Words were created by the teacher within the children's existing phonic knowledge. Children were encouraged to read the messages by blending the phonemes.

The children were highly motivated by the display and responded enthusiastically by writing messages to their alien friends using non-words. Children enjoyed writing these messages and reading them to one another and to the teacher. They eagerly awaited replies from the aliens at the beginning of each school day.

Applying new learning in the phonics lesson

In the final part of the phonics lesson, children should be given opportunities to apply their learning. This should be focused and relate to the new grapheme–phoneme correspondence and/or tricky word that has been taught in the main part of the lesson. The purpose of this part of the lesson is for children to read and/or write a sentence or a caption. This should

incorporate the grapheme/phoneme or tricky word which has been introduced in the lesson. The sentence or caption should be within the breadth of children's existing phonic knowledge. You can challenge the children to read a caption or sentence or you can challenge them to write a sentence or caption that has been dictated.

You need to be aware that children might not automatically apply their phonic knowledge and skills in their independent reading and writing outside the phonics lesson, even if they are able to demonstrate their ability to apply this learning within the phonics lesson. A good example of this is teaching children the tricky word *said*. As new learning in a phonics lesson, children are encouraged to focus on the phonetically plausible and tricky parts of the word. This is repeated throughout the lesson and consequently children are often able to read and spell the word during the lesson. However, beyond the lesson it is not uncommon for children to struggle to read or spell this word and they may revert to using phonetically plausible attempts in their independent writing (for example, *s-e-d*). During independent reading and writing, children are required to draw on a range of knowledge and skills they have been previously taught, whereas in phonics lessons there is a clear and much narrower focus which enables them to experience greater success. It is important that you do not devalue independent attempts at reading and writing. Much can be gleaned from assessing children's independent reading and writing. It is not unusual for there to be a disparity between assessments relating to a phonics lesson and those relating to independent reading and writing tasks.

CREATIVE APPROACH

You need to consider opportunities to engage children in applying their phonic knowledge, skills and understanding beyond the phonics lesson. Developing a discrete phonics area is obviously of great value. This area could include:

- previously taught grapheme–phoneme correspondences;
- new grapheme–phoneme correspondences;
- magnetic letters and magnetic boards;
- whiteboards and pens;
- glitter pens;
- letter tiles;
- jumbled sentences and captions relating to current stage of development in phonics;
- decodable texts which relate to current stage of development in phonics;
- phonics software;
- tricky word mats;
- words, captions and/or sentences relating to current stage of development in phonics.

In addition, you should also consider the wider learning environment. In a Foundation Stage classroom this could include a wide range of provision areas including role play, sand, water, creative areas, construction areas, malleable areas and small world areas. You need to think about how these areas could be enhanced to provide opportunities for children to apply their phonic knowledge and skills independently or through adult-supported play. The water area can be enhanced by adding ping-pong balls or flat pebbles to the water. On each ball or pebble you could write a separate grapheme, ensuring that there are multiples of some graphemes, particularly vowels. The graphemes should be within the children's existing phonic knowledge. The children can fish these out and put the graphemes together to make real and non-words. The children can independently make words of their own choice or the activity could be directed by you by giving them specific words which they must segment.

Developing a print-rich environment

Children will not automatically become competent readers or writers solely by immersing themselves in a daily discrete phonics lesson. You must ensure that you pay close attention to developing the learning environment to enable children to apply their phonic knowledge, skills and understanding. The following ideas are examples of how the learning environment can be enhanced to support young readers and writers.

- Classroom resources should be clearly labelled with text.

- Working areas (such as sand, water, creative areas) should be clearly labelled with text.

- Tricky words should be clearly displayed.

- Children's names should be displayed and opportunities should be planned to enable children to practise writing their own names independently.

- Greetings should be displayed in several languages including English.

- A display of days of the week should be prominent.

- A pictorial alphabet frieze should be visible.

- Text should be handwritten as well as word-processed.

- Displays should incorporate captions, sentences and questions from both teachers and children.

- Teachers should build a bank of familiar texts which children can reread.

- Shared texts should be clearly displayed.

- A range of attractive fiction and non-fiction text should be accessible to the children.

- Phonics games should be available, with consideration given to children's stage of development.

- Texts relating to past and present topic work should be accessible to the children.

- Decodable texts should be available for children to read independently, with consideration for children's stage of development in phonics.

- There should be texts with repetitive structures, rhyme and alliteration for children to read independently or to be read to them by a teacher.

- Opportunities for mark-making should be identified in the mark-making area.

- Develop a listening area for children to enjoy listening to stories, poems and rhymes.

- Consider the development of role-play areas and the use of puppets to re-enact stories and experiences.

- Ensure that there are opportunities for children to read and write in the outdoor area.

- Pay attention to the development of fine and gross motor skills, for example the use of ribbon sticks.

Critical questions

» *Teachers may not be in agreement with regard to displaying greetings in a range of languages. What are your views and why?*

» *Many teachers do not display all high-frequency words in areas which support children's development in writing. Some may only display tricky words. What might their reasons be for doing so?*

» *What are your views in relation to displaying tricky words only? What are your reasons for this?*

Developing indoor provision

In developing your indoor learning environment it is important to make all labelling (words, captions, sentences and questions) accessible to the children. This will require careful consideration on your part as only you will be aware of their phonic knowledge at any given time. When you create provision areas, provide the children with a wealth of opportunities to apply their phonic knowledge. Think carefully about how you can engage the children in blending phonemes, segmenting, reading and words. The value of a literate environment cannot be overstated and as you create each area of provision you need to carefully plan to facilitate the development of children's reading and writing. In planning your indoor learning environment you may wish to adopt some of the following suggestions:

- In each provision area, a 'Can you...?' provides the children with a possible focus for their play and learning. For example, in the malleable area, questions could be displayed such as *Can you press? Can you pull? Can you stretch? Can you print?*

- Create a central storage of a range of writing materials including paper, whiteboards, chalk mats, pencils, chalks, glitter pens, marker pens, felt-tip pens, biros, clipboards and charcoal. Children can access these resources freely and take them to any area of provision. This enables children to choose which materials they wish to use in specific areas rather than limiting the resources in a specific area to those chosen by the teacher.

Developing outdoor provision

Children are frequently motivated by a change in their learning environment. The outdoor environment can be used very effectively to deliver Systematic Synthetic Phonics. The outdoor provision provides children with opportunities to move freely, work on a larger scale, have fun and shout. You may wish to consider using the following resources as part of outdoor synthetic phonics lessons:

- chunky chalks for writing graphemes, words, captions and sentences;

- water and paintbrushes;

- ribbon sticks for gross motor development;

- sticks for writing graphemes and words in mud or sand;

- water pistols for 'shooting' specific graphemes or tricky words;

- long rolls of paper to write on with paint on the floor, on walls or fences;

- parachute games.

CASE STUDY

Sally was a final-year trainee working in a Reception class. She was keen to make her phonics lessons active and fun and wanted to maximise pupil participation. Sally decided to teach the lesson in the outdoor area. For the first part of the lesson, she placed some graphemes that children had been taught in hoops. These were laid out on the floor. Some of these were carefully selected because they included graphemes that the children had had difficulty with. Sally called out the corresponding phonemes and the children were asked to run to the appropriate grapheme. In the next part of the lesson Sally introduced the new grapheme–phoneme correspondence *oa*. She asked the children to write this in the air and they did this as Sally carefully modelled the formation of the letters. The children then practised writing this on the floor with chunky chalks. In the next part of the lesson, Sally shouted out words that incorporated *oa*. These included *boat, soap, oat, toad*. Using robot arms and legs, the children were asked to walk like a robot in response to each word that Sally shouted out. For example, in response to the word *boat* the children had to walk three paces, swinging their arms once every time they took a step. Sally had positioned a sand tray, glitter tray and soil tray in the outdoor area. The children also had access to a chalk board on the wall and chunky chalks for writing on the floor. Sally asked the children to choose where they wanted to work. She then shouted out words that incorporated the grapheme *oa*, and the children had to have a go at segmenting these by writing them in the various media. Finally Sally articulated a sentence to the children and they had to listen to this carefully and say it back to her. Sally had written this sentence on large cards. The cards were separate, and each word from the sentence was written on a separate card. The cards were jumbled up in the wrong order and the children were asked to work as a team to put the words in the correct order by laying the cards on the floor. Finally the children were asked to read the sentence back together and point to the grapheme *oa* in specific words.

- How did Sally maximise pupil participation in this lesson?

- Can you identify any potential issues that a lesson of this kind might throw up?

- Can you identify the four parts of the phonics lesson in this example?

Critical questions

In this chapter we have stressed the current focus of maximising pupil participation and limiting turn-taking opportunities and waiting time in lessons.

» *Do you agree with this current focus?*

» *What are the advantages and disadvantages of turn-taking?*

Critical reflection

We have emphasised an approach which makes effective use of visual, auditory and kinaesthetic channels because this approach will help to include all learners. However, while such an approach should maximise pupil participation and help to make your phonics lessons more effective, children need to apply their phonic knowledge and skills to reading and writing. Over-elaborate activities can distract children from the learning goal (Ofsted, 2010). Unless children learn to apply the learning from their phonics lessons to reading and writing, your teaching of phonics will not be effective. This is because the quality of teaching is judged by its impact on pupils' learning. The ultimate aim of phonics is to provide children with a tool to aid independence in reading and writing. If this does not happen, your phonics lessons are falling short of their goal. Children do not automatically apply their learning from one situation to another. Consequently, as much effort needs to go into teaching children how to apply their phonic knowledge and skills as is put into the teaching of phonics.

Critical points

» *A systematic approach to synthetic phonics requires all teachers within a school to follow an agreed programme which includes a clear teaching sequence.*

» *You must ensure that all children participate throughout all synthetic phonics lessons.*

» *You should adopt a multi-sensory approach to teaching synthetic phonics which draws on children's visual, auditory and kinaesthetic channels.*

» *Lessons should have a brisk pace.*

» *You should ensure that children are immersed in a literate learning environment.*

» *You should plan your lessons with a clear teaching focus which should be taught, practised and then applied.*

Taking it further

Jolliffe, W. (2007) *You Can Teach Phonics*. Leamington Spa: Scholastic.

6 Early reading

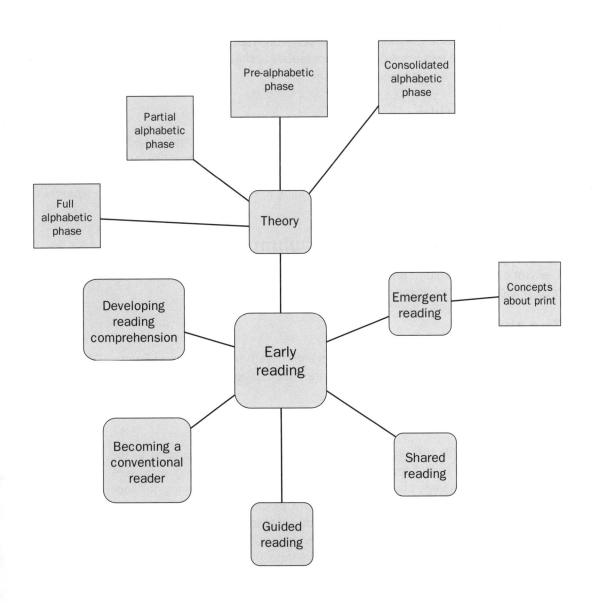

Links to the Early Years Foundation Stage

Communication and language: Listening and attention

The Early Years Foundation Stage states that children should be able to *listen to stories, accurately anticipating key events and respond to what they hear with relevant comments, questions or actions.*

Communication and language: Understanding

The Early Years Foundation Stage states that children should be able to *answer 'how' and 'why' questions ... in response to stories.*

Communication and language: Speaking

The Early Years Foundation Stage states that children should be able to *express themselves effectively, showing awareness of listeners' needs ... they develop their own narratives and explanations by connecting ideas or events.*

Literacy: Reading

The Early Years Foundation Stage states that by the end of this phase of education children should be able to *read and understand simple sentences. They use phonic knowledge to decode regular words and read them aloud accurately. They also read some common irregular words. They demonstrate understanding when talking with others about what they have read.*

Links to the National Curriculum

The National Curriculum promotes the use of Systematic Synthetic Phonics for word recognition and the importance of children reading for meaning.

The theory

Gough and Tunmer (1986) provide a model known as the Simple View of Reading. This model identifies two fundamental skills that children need to become fluent readers. These are:

- word recognition;

- language comprehension.

Successful reading is the product of both these skills. The separation of the two skills is useful because the model provides clear identification of the distinct processes of both word recognition and language comprehension, both of which are essential for fluency in reading as well as reading for meaning. Additionally, the separation of the two domains sends a clear signal to you, as the teacher, that different types of teaching support the distinct development of each skill. Word recognition processes are developed through decoding and the teaching of a sight vocabulary. You will develop these skills through your daily phonics lesson, and your pupils will apply them in guided, shared and independent reading tasks. Developing children's language comprehension necessitates a different approach. This will partly be developed through immersing children in a broad, rich language environment so that they are able to extend their vocabulary. Rich play-based learning environments, which facilitate social interaction, talk and communication, will facilitate the development of children's vocabulary. As a teacher you play a fundamental role in extending children's language development. Children need to be introduced to a wide range of vocabulary and understand its meaning. A communication-rich environment will support the development of language. Language comprehension is also developed through reading comprehension, which is explored later in this chapter. The development of word recognition is time-limited. It paves the way for children to read for meaning. You will find that some children are quite adept at reading the words on a page but have limited understanding of what they have read. Additionally some children may have good comprehension skills, in that they are able to respond to questions about stories that are read to them and are able to make predictions and retell stories. They may also have advanced vocabularies. However, these children may struggle with word recognition due to poor decoding skills and a poor sight vocabulary. You may find that some children have both poor word recognition and language comprehension and these children will require intervention in both aspects of their reading development. To become effective readers, children need to be skilled in both aspects. The model will enable you to identify which aspects need to be targeted in order to support children's development. The presentation of the model shows four quadrants and you will be able to identify which quadrant each child falls within. Some children may just require intervention in their word recognition skills through additional support with grapheme–phoneme correspondence and blending. Others, who may have mastered these skills, may require support to develop their reading comprehension or vocabulary development. Neither of these groups of children is reading effectively and they need different kinds of intervention to enable them to become effective readers.

It is helpful to understand theories of reading development to enable you to support children's word recognition skills. Ehri (1995) developed an influential model of reading development which shows how word recognition develops over time. The problem with models of development is that they often lead us to think that children's development is linear, when in reality it is complex and dynamic (Johnston and Watson, 2007). Ehri's model identifies four stages of reading development. These are:

- pre-alphabetic phase;
- partial alphabetic phase;
- full alphabetic phase;
- consolidated alphabetic phase.

The model provides a useful way of tracking children's development and should enable you to support them further.

Pre-alphabetic phase

Children's 'reading' at this stage is very visual and they can recognise words through their shapes, logos and colours of text. Many young children recognise the distinctive features of supermarket names. The context supports the young child in 'reading' such words. Without the context they would not be able to 'read' the word as they are only using visual cues rather than graphemes. Children at this stage of development are very aware of environmental print.

Partial alphabetic phase

At this stage of development a child has some understanding of phoneme–grapheme correspondence and its relationship to reading. However they have not mastered the skill of blending through all of the word and may just focus on the initial sound. Presented with the word *sun* they may say 'sand'. Children whose development is arrested at this stage may be at risk of becoming poor readers.

Full alphabetic phase

At this stage of development, a child is able to blend the sounds throughout a word to read it. A child will see s-u-n and read *sun*. Presented with phonetically irregular words they will apply a degree of phonic knowledge to read them. To become competent readers, children will need to fully master this phase in their reading development.

Consolidated alphabetic phase

At this stage, children can recognise larger units of sound and will break words into smaller units of sound to read them. For example, presented with the word *pulling*, a child will read *pull* and *ing* and blend the two units of words together. Once a child has reached this level of reading development they can apply their skills to read any 'new' words.

Emergent reading

Children develop an awareness of environmental print from a very early age. They are surrounded by signs, logos and notices and they quickly begin to associate these with meaning. Children's awareness of print gradually expands as they are exposed to magazines, newspapers and books in the home environment. Children who are raised in a literate home environment are more likely to become good readers. Some children, unfortunately, are brought up in print-impoverished environments and this can have detrimental effects on their subsequent reading development.

Palaiologou (2010) discusses how a child moves from being a naïve reader to a more expert reader. Initially children may 'read' the pictures, but later in their development they start to pay more attention to the text. At the emergent stage of reading, the crucial foundations for subsequent reading development are laid. Initially children start to understand that books are different to toys, and very young babies enjoy sharing picture books with adults. It is never too early to instil a respect for books in children. Books have a clear purpose and should be valued and enjoyed. Storing them separately, while also making them accessible, will facilitate an early love of literature.

As children develop they begin to understand how books work. It is at this stage that children will start to interact with books by turning the pages, pointing to pictures and naming objects.

As their participation increases they will grow to enjoy listening to and joining in with stories. Children enjoy repetitive texts and this facilitates their participation in story-telling. Gradually they will be able to retell stories, recognise and name familiar characters and re-enact scenes from stories. They will begin to develop their own stories using pictures as a stimulus. Developing an attractive book area will engender a love of books in children. This should include:

- predictable texts;
- counting books;
- rhyming texts;
- non-fiction texts;
- traditional tales;
- cumulative tales;
- nursery rhymes;
- big books;
- story sacks;
- puppets;
- story CDs;
- books produced by children.

Young children are attracted to the illustrations on the front of books and glean a great deal of information, relating to the content of the book, from these illustrations. For this reason we recommend that books are displayed with the front covers clearly visible.

Concepts about print

Within the emergent stage, children will begin to develop a more in-depth understanding of text. Marie Clay used the term 'concepts about print' to indicate the level of knowledge and understanding that children need to acquire before they are able to become good readers. These concepts provide the necessary foundations for subsequent reading development and include:

- understanding directionality – text is read from left to right and top to bottom;
- identifying letters;
- identifying words;
- naming punctuation;
- understanding the function of punctuation;
- understanding book orientation;

- identifying the front and back cover;
- identifying the title;
- identifying the spine;
- understanding that it is the print that communicates the meaning;
- recognising inverted print;
- recognising when letters are transposed in words;
- identifying anagrams;
- understanding that correct word ordering results in meaning;
- understanding the concept of first and last;
- understanding the difference between upper and lower case letters.

These concepts about print are an intrinsic part of assessing children's development in reading. As children read, in a variety of contexts, including shared, guided and individual reading, you must take the opportunity to focus carefully on the concepts they understand as well as those that need to be developed. It is too easy to overlook these basic concepts which are fundamental to becoming an effective reader.

As children's phonemic knowledge develops, they will start to blend phonemes to decode words. It is at this stage that children's comprehension may be impeded. As children focus on the smallest units of sound within words, they may not internalise the meaning of the text. However, it is important to remember that decoding is a time-limited strategy. It unlocks the door to deciphering print and, once acquired, children will be able to focus more on reading for meaning. Certainly, without decoding skills, children will not be able to understand text. The Simple View of Reading demonstrates that the skills of word recognition and those of language comprehension should be developed concurrently, even though the emphasis in the early stages of development should be on word recognition. Consequently, while children are focusing on decoding, you need to ensure that the development of their comprehension skills is not neglected. Strategies for developing reading comprehension will be explored later in this chapter.

It is at the emergent stage of reading that children start to interact with books and develop their interest in literature. In the early stages of emergent reading, children can often be observed pretending to read, drawing on their experiences of sharing books with adults as well as their knowledge of the concepts of print. This should be encouraged and valued. You should also provide children with opportunities to share books with one another.

Becoming a conventional reader

When children have mastered the skill of decoding, it remains important that teachers continue to read individually with each child. There is a fundamental difference between listening to a child reading and teaching a child to read. When conducting individual reading conferences with children, you should carefully consider the following.

- Ensure that children are competently blending to read unfamiliar words, and offer support when this is not the case.

- Use *pause, prompt, praise*: initially give the child time to address the encountered challenge, then offer pertinent prompts to support the reader and finally praise their attempts.

- Individual reading conferences enable you to focus the children's attention and specific concepts about print. For example you may wish to draw their attention to the purpose and effect of punctuation.

- Individual reading conferences also enable you to draw a child's attention to the vocabulary choices of the author by discussing the effects of specific words and phrases (reading as a writer).

- This is an opportunity to develop children's comprehension skills by teaching a range of comprehension strategies.

Conventional readers should have access to a wide range of reading materials. These include decodable texts, reading scheme texts, access to free choice books, children's newspapers and magazines. A range of non-fiction materials should also be available.

Ideally you will have the support of parents and carers who will read with their children at home, and this should be encouraged. However, in some schools this can be a challenge. Parents may not be literate themselves, they may only be literate in their home language or they may simply not value books and reading. Under these circumstances you will need to consider the ways in which you can provide additional support for children in school if they do not regularly access books at home with their parents and carers. Various support mechanisms can be employed and these can include:

- paired reading – a more able reader is partnered with a child who requires further support, to promote the enjoyment of reading as opposed to teaching reading skills;

- providing additional opportunities for these children to read with you or other adults individually;

- providing additional group intervention for children who need further support with reading.

You will need to ensure that you plan opportunities to conduct reading conferences with children. This will be a significant challenge because you cannot conduct reading conferences when you are teaching mathematics, for example. However, there should be times during the week when children are set independent tasks and this will enable you to work individually with children on reading. Teaching reading is one of the most important things that you will do as a teacher of young children. Consequently, it is not something that should be solely delegated to teaching assistants. Many teaching assistants are highly qualified in the teaching of reading but some are not. Reading is a complex skill and the teaching of reading should always be overseen by a professional who has the knowledge, skills and understanding to further children's development. Reading unlocks the door to the rest of the curriculum and consequently its development cannot be left to chance.

Critical questions

» *To what extent can a focus on decoding print result in children not reading for meaning?*

» *What are the arguments for and against reading scheme books?*

» *What are the arguments for and against decodable books?*

» *What are the arguments for and against paired reading?*

Developing reading comprehension

In order to become fluent readers, children must understand what they read. You should not assume that this is an automatic process – indeed you will discover that it is not – and children need to be taught a range of reading comprehension strategies. Comprehension is essentially about gaining meaning from text. In order to do this children need to:

*   understand the text;

*   engage with the text;

*   respond to the text;

*   critically evaluate the text.

Reading comprehension should be an active process and children make better progress when you teach them the strategies. This will involve explicit instruction during shared, guided and independent reading opportunities. Children who can automatically decode words, and have a good sight vocabulary of tricky words, are in a better position to focus on deducing meaning from text.

Fundamentally children need to acquire the skill of prediction. You should engage them in considering what might happen next in a story and also encourage them to give reasons for their responses. Children should be encouraged to return to the text to check the accuracy of their predictions. They need to share their predictions with their peers, either in groups or with talk partners. Children can be given the opportunity to consider story characters by listening to initial character descriptions and texts and using this information to produce a drawing. Once they have listened and internalised the text in its entirety, they can return to their drawing and add descriptive words or phrases related to the character based on the information they have gleaned.

Skilled questioning is essential to develop children's understanding of text. Closed factual questions (literal questions) will help to assess a child's ability to recall information. These questions often have only one answer. Examples include:

*   what is the name of the dog?

*   where does the story take place?

*   how many characters are there?

However, this type of questioning does not facilitate the development of higher-order reading skills, such as the ability to use inference and deduction or to be critical about what they have read. The development of these skills is dependent on open-ended questioning, and examples of these questions include:

- what do we know about the setting?

- what do you know about the character?

- how does this story make you feel? Why?

- what do you see in your mind when you read this story/poem?

- why does the writer use this word ? (Reading as a writer)

- who is the most important character?

- did you enjoy this book? Why/why not?

- what is your favourite part?

- what is the effect of this word/punctuation/use of alliteration? (Reading as a writer)

During shared, guided and independent reading opportunities it is essential that you plan questions that will appropriately meet the needs of your learners. Questions should be differentiated. As a general rule begin by including closed questions, and introduce more open-ended questioning as reading skills develop. It is also important to develop questioning further by asking deductive or inferential questions which require children to read between the lines rather than simply extract information from the text. Children should also be encouraged to ask their own questions which can be responded to by peers as well as adults. Engaging children in group discussions where they can share different viewpoints is beneficial in encouraging children to support their opinions.

Bloom's Taxonomy shows higher- and lower-order levels of thinking. Questioning can be related to the levels of thinking in this framework as follows:

1 **Knowledge** – Who? What? Where? When? How? *Where did the story take place?*

2 **Comprehension** – Explanations relating to the text. *Why do you think the giant was angry?*

3 **Application** – Finding several examples in the text to support a response. *Can you tell me the different ways in which Goldilocks was naughty?*

4 **Analysis** – What is the evidence for …? *What kind of character was the wolf? How do you know this?*

5 **Synthesis** – *What similarities and differences are there in these two versions of the story?*

6 **Evaluation** – *What do you feel about this story and why?*

Reading comprehension strategies should be taught through a range of text types, including non-fiction texts. Children need to understand how non-fiction texts work and should be taught the skills of:

- locating information using the contents page;

- retrieving information from glossaries;

- using an index;

- using titles and subtitles to locate information;

- extracting information from tables, diagrams and charts.

Children must also be taught that non-fiction texts do not necessarily need to be read in their entirety.

Young children need to develop the skill of retelling stories. This can be done in a range of ways which include:

- the use of story maps or story boards which enable children to sequence the events of a story using pictures and/or captions;

- presenting children with pictures from a story which they can sequence and later develop further by including connectives including *first, then, later, next, finally*, between each picture;

- presenting children with jumbled text of stories which they are required to sequence in the correct order;

- using a story-teller's chair when the children become story-tellers.

Further reading comprehension strategies can include the following:

- reading sections of a text and stopping to allow children to summarise their understanding;

- text marking – underlining or highlighting parts of the text for significant purposes. For example, find all the words that describe a character;

- encouraging children to refer to and make dictionaries/word books to develop their understanding of words;

- ranking characters in a story from the meanest to the kindest;

- sorting statements about a story into those that are true and those that are false;

- sorting statements from the story into those that are factual and those that are opinions;

- comparing the information gained from both texts and illustrations. Illustrations can offer additional detail to that gleaned from texts;

- retelling stories from the viewpoint of different characters;

- when a character in a story faces a problem stop reading and encourage the children to resolve it before returning to the text;

- considering the best and worst parts of the story;

- encouraging the children to consider what they would do if they were placed in the role of a character faced with specific circumstances;

- writing a blurb for a book;

- completing thought and speech bubbles to indicate what a character may be thinking or saying;

- completing book reviews;

- comparing several versions of the same story and noting similarities and differences;

- transposing a story from one genre to another;

- using drama strategies to develop children's understanding of stories – we referred to some key strategies in Chapter 2.

Shared reading

Shared reading provides you with an opportunity to model being a reader and the reading process. You will need to locate enlarged text (big books) as well as texts for display on the interactive whiteboard. Shared reading is usually carried out with the whole class, although it can take place with a small group of children. We do not want to stipulate a specific model for the teaching of shared reading because all teachers will develop different methods for different purposes. However, you might find it helpful to consider the following points.

- Ensure that all children can see the text.

- Introduce the book: read the blurb with the children; look at the title; identify the author; discuss what the book might be about, drawing on the illustrations if appropriate.

- Start reading the text, pointing accurately at each word as you read it, encouraging the children to participate where appropriate.

- Model turning the pages, reading from left to right and top to bottom.

- Ask questions as you read to check the children's comprehension using a range of comprehension strategies as discussed in this chapter.

- Draw the children's attention to the specific structural features of the text type, for example the use of time connectives in recounts and the numbering systems in instructional texts.

- Have a clear focus for the teaching. For example, if the focus of the lesson is for children to identify rhyme in the text, focus your questioning on this aspect of the text.

- Ensure that questioning is differentiated to meet the needs of all learners. This may include both open and closed questioning.

Once the children are familiar with the shared text it is essential that this is accessible to them so that they can interact with the text independently beyond the lesson. Whenever possible, the choice of a shared text should relate to other aspects of the children's learning. A range of text types should be accessed including poetry, fiction and non-fiction.

Guided reading

Guided reading is an invaluable opportunity to meet the common reading needs of a group of children, and for this reason texts must be selected with the learning needs of a group of children in mind. It must be at the appropriate level for the group, and the lesson should have a specific learning focus. You may wish to develop the children's skills in sequencing a story and therefore this is an opportunity for this skill to be the focus of the lesson. For more able readers it may be appropriate to focus on developing their skills in inference and deduction. Again we do not wish to advocate a specific model for teaching, but you may wish to consider the following.

- Ensure that each child has their own copy of the chosen text.

- Give the children time to explore the text.

- Together discuss the title, author, blurb and predict what the text may be about.

- Draw the children's attention to any unfamiliar words.

- Remind the children of strategies to decode words if applicable.

- Provide the children with an opportunity to read the text individually (we do not advocate a 'round robin' approach) and at their own pace.

- As the children read, take the opportunity to assess their reading skills and intervene to offer individual support as highlighted through your observations.

- Children will finish reading the text at different times and it is your responsibility to extend their learning so that they do not spend time waiting while other children are still reading.

- Once each child in the group has finished reading the text it is important that they return to the focus of the lesson and demonstrate their learning. If the focus of the lesson was to develop children's understanding of sequencing then this should be revisited in the plenary.

The purpose of guided reading sessions is to teach a group of children with a shared and specific learning need. In addition, they provide each child with an opportunity to apply their phonic knowledge. We have advised you against using the 'round robin' approach, for several reasons. First, while one child is reading, the others are often simply waiting and may not fully engage with the text. Secondly, this approach limits the amount of text that each child is able to read. Additionally, children can feel pressurised as they await their turn. Some children do not enjoy reading aloud in front of their peers and this should be acknowledged.

CASE STUDY

Charlie was a final-year trainee teacher working in a Reception class. She felt that her guided reading sessions were becoming too predictable. She decided to consider using the outdoor area to teach this aspect of the curriculum. She developed a treasure hunt in the outdoor provision by hiding written clues in various places. The children were required to find the clues, read them and use them to find the hidden treasure. Each clue indicated where to find the next clue, and the final clue led to the treasure.

• What other approaches could you use to make guided reading less predictable?

Critical question

» What are the arguments for and against guided reading?

CREATIVE APPROACH

The outdoor area can be developed with the use of story dens. Shelters can be created to provide quiet spaces for children to read stories individually and in pairs in the outdoors. Positioning a 'story-teller's chair' in the outdoors provides children with an opportunity to share their own oral narratives or retellings of stories they have heard with each other.

Teaching a lesson in role as a character is an exciting way to develop children's reading comprehension skills. The children could be invited to ask you questions and you could answer them as the character.

CASE STUDY

Madhu was teaching a Year 1 class on her final teaching placement. The children had been reading the story of *Little Red Riding Hood*. Madhu decided to teach a lesson in role as a way of getting the children to ask their own questions. She started the lesson as herself. Suddenly, there was a knock on the door and the teaching assistant told Madhu that there was an urgent message for her in the school office. Madhu left the room immediately and left the class with the teaching assistant. Madhu returned to the classroom dressed as Little Red Riding Hood. Nervously, she told the children that she had got lost in the woods and had ended up in their classroom. The children were amazed and invited her into the classroom. They allowed her to sit in their teacher's chair and started to ask her lots of questions: *What was it like meeting a wolf? Why did you go in the woods on your own? What was it like in the woods?* The children were completely engaged. Little Red Riding Hood then asked the children if they would do some simple jobs for her to help her on her way home. The tasks all related to the story and provided a purposeful context for learning.

• Read *Little Red Riding Hood*. What tasks might Madhu have planned to provide purposeful contexts for reading, writing, speaking and listening?

INTERNATIONAL PERSPECTIVES

Finland's approach to early education focuses on developing children's social, moral and physical development, and less emphasis is placed on reading and phonics. By the age of 15, Finnish children outperform their English counterparts and display better attitudes to reading. Could it be that the focus on laying important foundations for learning in the early years is more beneficial in the long term than focusing on the formal teaching of reading?

Critical reflection

The importance of children developing phonological awareness as a pre-requisite skill for reading is clearly embedded in the new Early Years Foundation Stage. The framework emphasises the importance of children having early knowledge of rhyme, rhythm and alliteration. It also emphasises the importance of emergent reading, concepts about print and early phonemic awareness. However, a fundamental skill in reading is the ability to visually discriminate between graphemes. Early visual discrimination is not emphasised in the framework as a pre-requisite skill for reading. How important do you consider this skill to be in reading development?

Critical points

This chapter has emphasised:

» the importance of providing an enabling learning environment which facilitates the development of reading, particularly the emergent stage of reading;

» the importance of children developing familiarity with key concepts about print;

» the difference between teaching children to read and listening to readers;

» the Simple View of Reading and its application to practice;

» the importance of reading for meaning and reading comprehension strategies.

Taking it further

Ehri, L.C. (1995) Phases of Development in Learning to Read by Sight. *Journal of Research in Reading*, 18, (2): 116–125.

Ofsted (2010) *Reading by Six: How the Best Schools do it*. London: Ofsted.

7 Early writing

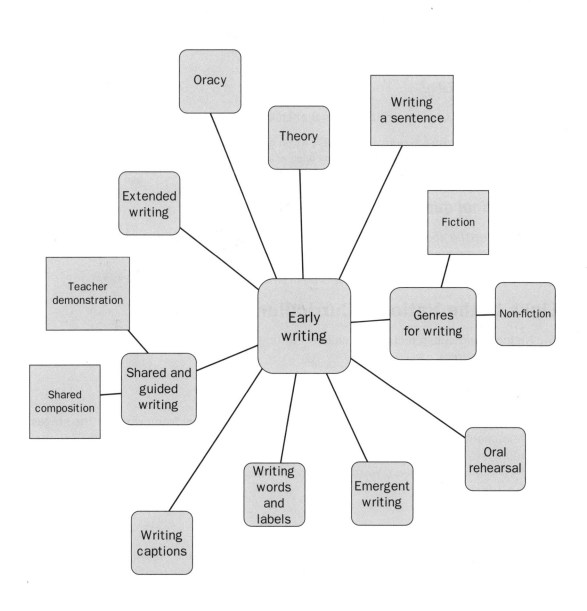

Links to the Early Years Foundation Stage

Communication and language: Listening and attention

The Early Years Foundation Stage states that children need to listen to stories, anticipate key events and respond to what they hear and give attention to others.

Communication and language: Understanding

The Early Years Foundation Stage states that children should be able to respond to 'how' and 'why' questions in response to stories and events.

Communication and language: Speaking

The Early Years Foundation Stage states that children should be able to develop their own narratives and explanations by connecting ideas or events.

Literacy: Writing

The Early Learning Goal for writing states that children should be able to

use their phonic knowledge to write words in ways which match their spoken sounds. They also write some irregular common words. They write simple sentences which can be read by themselves and others. Some words are spelt correctly and others are phonetically plausible.

Critical questions

» *How do the above expectations underpin the skills needed for children to become effective writers?*

» *Do you think the Early Learning Goal in writing is an appropriate expectation?*

Links to the National Curriculum

The National Curriculum focuses on children writing for a range of purposes and audiences in a range of genres.

The theory

Over 20 years ago Nicholls et al. (1989) produced a theoretical framework for the stages of development in writing. The levels within this framework do not relate to National Curriculum levels of achievement, but the model is a useful framework which will help you to understand how children's writing develops. The stages in the model are summarised in Figure 1 (opposite).

Oracy

Oral language development is rooted in the early sounds and interactions of babies. Children will develop communication skills at different rates, and as a practitioner you play a

Stage of development in writing	Characteristics of children's writing	What you can do to support children's development
Level 1: Orientation towards writing	• Scribble text – exploring the possibilities of mark-making implements. • Scribble which incorporates invented symbols. • Scribble and drawings. • Scribbles/drawings and recognisable letters and numbers. • Whole words incorporated into scribble/drawings or random letters.	• Value children's attempts at writing and encourage them to read it to you. • Focus on helping the children to understand the difference between a word and a picture. • Observe children writing to see if they can: control the writing implement; work from left to right; leave spaces between words; write some high-frequency words; and use knowledge of grapheme–phoneme correspondence to write simple words, focusing on use of initial sound. Use observations to inform planning.
Level 2: Early text making	• Writing which children can read to the teacher which includes some conventional letters.	• Model segmentation during shared writing. • Model spacing between words. • Model letter formation. • Teach a bank of sight words and ask children to practise writing these. • Develop understanding of a sentence.
Level 3: Initial independent writing	• Simple texts which can be partly read by others. • Ability to organise words into sentences. • Ability to spell some familiar words using knowledge of sound and sight recognition.	• Model uses of punctuation in shared reading and writing. • Model linking sentences in shared reading and writing. • Extend repertoire of spellings.
Level 4: Associate writing	• Accurate and fluent texts. • Use of punctuation. • Use of conventional spelling patterns. • Ability to link sentences.	• Model the features of different text types. • In shared and guided reading expose children to different genres. • In shared writing model composition of different text types. • Teach complex sentences.
Beyond level 4	• Texts using the structural and language features of different genres. • More complex sentences.	• Model the process of drafting, editing, redrafting.

Figure 1: *A model of writing development (adapted from Nicholls, 1989).*

fundamental role in facilitating the development of these skills. Children need to confidently use language to communicate before they will be able to write. Children's language can be developed through interactions with adults and each other. You can support the development of these skills in a range of ways. These must include:

- spending time talking to and having conversations with babies and children;

- providing rich play-based learning that will facilitate social interaction and communication and using these as opportunities to extend children's language and communication;

- seizing opportunities for sustained shared thinking;

- developing a language- and communication-rich enabling environment;

- identifying children's needs in relation to language and communication and planning to support subsequent development in relation to these;

- modelling speaking in complete sentences;

- providing children with opportunities to ask their own questions.

Poor language and communication disadvantages children, frequently resulting in low achievement in literacy. Children who are able to articulate a sentence are better prepared to write in sentences. Children who can develop oral narratives will subsequently be able to transfer these skills to producing written narratives. Children with broader experiences of language will have a wider range of vocabulary to draw upon in their writing. Varied, rich, stimulating and meaningful experiences underpin subsequent successes in writing. Children are able to draw on such experiences as they develop as writers. Some children will be immersed in rich language and communication experiences in their formative years. However, other children may be raised in language-impoverished environments which inevitably impede their development in language and communication. These children will require your expertise to support and enhance their development.

Emergent writing

Children must acquire controlled gross motor skills as a pre-requisite to the fine motor skills needed to become effective writers. It is essential that you assess the development of each child's gross motor skills and engage them in activities to further develop these as is necessary. Ensure that such activities are enjoyable and provide children with a range of opportunities to practise their gross motor movements. These activities could include:

- the use of ribbon sticks using one hand – most children will select their dominant hand;

- the use of ribbon sticks using two hands;

- using broad brushes and paints to make marks using one hand then two hands;

- using chunky chalks to make marks;

- making patterns in the air with one hand, then two hands, then with a finger – patterns could be free movements in response to music, then could become more refined, using shapes;

- using sticks or fingers to make marks in sand, glitter, soil or gravel.

Once children are using controlled gross motor movements, you can begin to focus on developing their fine motor skills. Initially you must not be pressurised into rushing the children into using pencil and paper to make marks, although these should be available. Fine motor skills can be developed, for example, using tweezers in a range of sizes to pick up objects of various sizes. Children can be gradually introduced to manipulating and building with simple construction materials with smaller components. Threading various-sized beads onto laces is another excellent way of developing fine motor skills.

Children need to be introduced to a wide range of mark-making materials and they need opportunities to explore how to use these. You should work alongside children to model the ways in which the different mark-making tools can be used. Children's exposure to these tools will lead to their developing greater control in the use of them.

During the emergent stage of writing, many children view themselves as 'writers'. This should be encouraged and celebrated. Children do not follow a clear developmental path as they learn to write. You may see many, but not all, of the following characteristics in children's early attempts as 'writers':

- random marks;

- simple drawings which show increasing control;

- combination of drawings and marks and/or recognisable graphemes;

- repeated patterns;

- attempts to copy features of writing they have seen, including lists and lines of writing;

- the appearance of recognisable but random letters or graphemes;

- letters from their own names;

- an emerging ability to produce graphemes and articulate the corresponding phoneme;

- inconsistent letter formation and mixed upper and lower case letters;

- children's attempts to 'read' what they have written and ascribe meaning to their marks;

- a developing understanding that, in English, print is written and read from left to right and top to bottom.

At this stage you need to work alongside children to model the different purposes for writing. All areas of provision in the setting should offer opportunities for children to mark-make and write, and your role in scaffolding these skills cannot be overstated. Children need to see you as a writer, and you need to demonstrate the purposes of writing within different contexts. At this stage, children are clearly 'writers' and it is your responsibility to further develop these skills. Children's attempts at mark-making provide evidence of their development in writing, and in your placements you should collect and carefully analyse the independent writing that children have produced and use this as a basis for planning the next steps in learning for each child.

Children will continue to benefit from working alongside adults to further develop their skills as writers. These should include:

- effectively holding a writing implement;
- writing their own name using upper and lower case letters appropriately;
- learning to form letters correctly.

Emergent writing is the foundation for developing children's self-concepts and confidence about being a writer. It is vital that their development is nurtured and celebrated. Much damage can de done if children's early attempts at writing are devalued. Disregarding children's early independent attempts to write can have significant and long-lasting effects on their subsequent attitudes towards writing.

Writing words and labels

As children become more competent and develop their understanding of phoneme–grapheme correspondence, opportunities should be created for them to write simple regular words. If they are supported and encouraged they should be able to make phonetically plausible attempts at more complex words. It is at this stage that you should be able to create purposes to enable them to apply these newly acquired skills. A purposeful inroad into encouraging children to write words at this stage of their development is to introduce labels. There must be a clear purpose for the labels, which could include:

- labelling objects for an interactive display;
- labelling classroom resources;
- labelling models that they have made;
- scientific labels relating to materials – *shiny, dull, wood, metal, plastic*, etc.

It is important to draw children's attention to labels on display in the learning environment so that children begin to develop an awareness of their purpose.

Phonics lessons will have introduced the children to some tricky words. These are the only words that need to be displayed and accessible to the children. They should be encouraged to make phonetically plausible attempts to write all other words. Encouraging them to do so will offer you an invaluable insight into children's achievements and future learning needs.

Children's attempts at writing words will vary enormously. Some may write single letters. Others will write groups of letters and some letters may be omitted. These attempts will enable you to assess each child's ability to hear the order of the phonemes in each word and to offer targeted support in this area.

Writing captions

The learning environment should include simple captions that convey meaning to the children and which wherever possible should be derived from the children's current phonic knowledge. Again, children's attention must be drawn to these captions. They should not be seen as wallpaper, and their meaning and purpose must be clear.

Children need to see adults writing captions. This can be achieved through shared writing as well as working alongside children. You need to emphasise that each caption must make sense if it is to have a purpose. Displays of children's work relating to current learning often provide an effective stimulus for writing captions. Ideas from the children should be encouraged and the caption should initially be written by the practitioner with the children, as a shared writing opportunity.

Phonics lessons provide an opportunity for children to write simple captions created and spoken by you. These should relate directly to the focus of the lesson.

Children's independent attempts at writing captions should be encouraged. They will independently write captions in the mark-making area as well as other areas of provision. Additionally, children might write captions for classroom displays or class books. They also enjoy adding captions to their own drawings.

Writing a sentence

Initially you will have to model a process which will support children in writing a simple sentence. This can be done through shared writing and you may find the following steps helpful.

Think it – model thinking of a sentence in your head.

Say it – say the sentence out loud several times and ask the children to check for meaning.

Write it – encourage the children to support you in writing the words in the correct order.

Read it – check that the written sentence matches the spoken sentence.

In shared writing, children's contributions to the writing process should be sought. Children can be challenged to think of their own sentence and you can scribe this with their support.

You can dictate simple sentences during your phonics lessons and challenge children to make attempts at writing them down. These sentences must relate to the focus of the lesson.

The process above can also be used during guided writing sessions in which there should be a clear focus for learning. Shared and guided writing are explained later in this chapter.

Some children may struggle to develop their understanding that a sentence needs to make sense. To support them in developing this understanding you can support them in reading a simple sentence. You can then present the same sentence to them as single words which they must then re-order. It is a useful activity to demonstrate that when the words are in the wrong order no meaning can be derived from the sentence.

Sentences should be displayed in the learning environment and there should always be opportunities for children to write independently. With plenty of opportunities for children to develop their early writing skills through guided and shared writing, they should begin to develop the confidence to write simple sentences independently. These attempts should be valued and they will also provide you with an assessment opportunity to identify their next steps. These next steps will become a focus for guided and shared work in the immediate future. Children need to be involved in assessing their own sentences against clear success criteria. These may include leaving spaces between each word in a sentence, demarcating sentences with a capital letter and a full stop, and ensuring that the sentence makes sense. Success criteria will vary from child to child, and many children will not be able to focus on more than one criterion at a time. Children should be reminded about their personal writing targets before they start to write and they should have the opportunity to evaluate their work against these. You should praise the child's attempts, and feedback should be focused and relate to the success criteria. You should then communicate 'next steps' to the children.

CASE STUDY

Tara was undertaking her final school-based placement in a Reception class. In one literacy lesson she wanted to focus on the features of a sentence. Through shared writing she modelled the process of think it, say it, write it, read it. The sentence related to a class theme. She then provided the children with an opportunity to think of their own sentence in pairs. Following several suggestions from the children, Tara chose a sentence suggested by one pair of children, and with the support of the class she modelled how to write this sentence. Tara reiterated the features of a sentence and she listed these on the board. She told the class that she wanted to see these features in their independent work. The whole-class input was followed with an independent activity where the children were asked to write a sentence relating to a specific focus. In the plenary, Tara used the visualiser to display one child's attempt at writing a sentence. She reminded the children about the features of a sentence. With the example of work up on the screen, Tara then asked *Does this sentence begin with a capital letter? Show me with your thumbs*. In response the children were required to peer-assess the work. She then repeated this process with the next feature: *Is there a finger space between each word?* Again, she asked the children to peer-assess the work. She continued this process until all the features had been covered. Finally she asked the class to say one good thing about the child's work and to identify an EBI – *even better if*. This required the class to generate a target for improving the work.

- What aspects of good practice can you identify in this case study?
- What issues can you identify?

Extended writing

Children need a broad range of skills before they can write independently. These include:

- an awareness of sentence structure and sentence components;
- an ability to spell monosyllabic words to attempt new words;
- a degree of fine motor control.

Although a child may have acquired many of these skills, this is not sufficient for them to be able to confidently produce independent pieces of writing. To write independently you must share a purpose for the task with the children. The children will write more effectively if they know why they have been asked to write. In addition, their writing will be richer if they have ideas and experiences upon which they can draw. Giving children clear purposes for writing must be well considered. It is not sufficient to ask children to write just because you want them to. They will be more motivated if they have a clear purpose for doing so.

CASE STUDY

Purposes for writing

The children were familiar with the story of *Jack and the Beanstalk*. They had listened to it, read it, re-enacted it and retold it using pictures and puppets. Following these experiences the teacher engaged the children in different purposes for writing, dependent upon their abilities. A stimulus for the activity was presented through a letter to the class from Jack and his mother explaining that they wished to celebrate their newly found wealth with a party. The children in the class were invited to help Jack and his mother prepare for the forthcoming party. One group was asked to write a shopping list of food for the party. Another group was asked to produce invitations for the party. One group wrote a set of instructions to enable Jack and his mother to make egg sandwiches. Another followed a set of oral instructions to make strawberry mousse.

- How did the listening activity relate to writing?
- Why do you think the teacher did not involve all the children in just one of the activities?

As a stimulus for writing during the Christmas period, the teacher produced a letter from Father Christmas which was shared with the children. During the previous night he had called into the school for a cup of hot chocolate and had inadvertently left a sack of presents behind. It was a sack of presents for another school. Father Christmas remembered where he had left it and one of the children was asked to locate it and bring it back to the classroom. As the sack was brought into the classroom it created great excitement among the children. Father Christmas enlisted the help of the children in his preparations for Christmas. He had wrapped all the presents and he had forgotten what was inside them. One group was asked to feel the parcels and then write labels to attach to the parcels. The second problem was that Father Christmas had no idea what to give the head teacher for Christmas. Another group was asked to write a list of suggestions for what she might like. Father Christmas asked another group to write him a letter to tell him what they would like him to bring them for Christmas when he returned to collect his sack.

- Consider how you could provide differentiated tasks using a different stimulus.

- Consider how you might cater within these tasks for a group of children who are currently at the very early stages of phonemic awareness.

CREATIVE APPROACH

Inspiring young writers

Children will be more motivated to write if they are stimulated to do so. Stimuli could include:

- photographs;
- DVD clips;
- first-hand experiences;
- objects;
- stories;
- drama.

Without a stimulus for writing, many children will struggle to generate ideas and they may lack motivation. Drama is a particularly powerful experience for writing. It can provide children with opportunities to enter into imaginary worlds and they can subsequently draw upon these in their own writing. Children will often generate richer vocabulary through drama, which can then be transferred to their independent writing. Drama also provides children with valuable opportunities to share ideas with their peers and to use and extend these ideas in their own work.

Children need to write for a range of audiences. Children could:

- write a story for a younger child;
- write a letter to the head teacher suggesting simple developments within the school;
- write simple book reviews for their peers;
- write messages to characters in story books;
- write extracts of speech in speech bubbles attached to characters for their peers to read;
- write letters to children in other schools or in other countries;
- write captions for a class book to go in the class library.

Children will be supported to produce more extended pieces of writing through a range of shared and guided writing activities. You will need to plan regular opportunities to enable you to model the skills of being a writer. Shared and guided writing activities should have a clear focus based on class, group and individual needs.

Children should be given opportunities to pursue their own interests and you need to plan to incorporate these into writing activities. Find out about the interests of children within your class and capitalise on these to motivate children to write. Boys can be more challenging to engage in writing. Exploiting their interests in superhero play by designing purposes for writing around these stimuli can be a successful motivator for writing.

You must not confine writing materials to paper and pencils alone. Writing implements can often be vital in motivating children to write and some children may prefer to write

- using glitter pens;
- on whiteboards;
- on the computer/I-Pad using word-processing software;
- in different-coloured pens or pencils.

Initially you should encourage the children to write freely and you should celebrate their independent attempts. When evaluating children's work with them, targets should be specific and achievable. Often it is better to get them to focus on one thing at a time. Children cannot be expected to focus on sentence structure, punctuation, spelling, handwriting and content together. Based on your knowledge of each child, you need to identify achievable, realistic targets which you can subsequently monitor. As children gain in confidence they will increasingly be able to evaluate their own work and generate their own targets. Do not focus on correcting all spelling errors as this will demotivate children. It is more productive to focus on one repetitive error by identifying it and asking the child to work on it. Once children are confident writers, you can increasingly start to focus on spelling, punctuation and grammar. However, in the early stages children need to enjoy writing, and their attempts should be praised rather than crushed.

Oral rehearsal

Children should be given opportunities to orally rehearse their writing before they put pencil (or any other writing implement) to paper. This will enable them to think through their ideas before committing them to paper. Children should also be given the opportunity to orally rehearse their writing with a peer (response partner) before starting to write. The advantage of this is that children can then receive feedback from their peers to enhance the quality of their ideas. During this process, children should *write as a reader*: they should consider the impact of their ideas and language choices on the reader. This process is ongoing throughout the subsequent writing activity.

Genres for writing

Children need to be introduced to a range of genres for writing including fiction and non-fiction texts. Through shared reading you should introduce children to models of different types, drawing attention to the specific structural features and language choices of each genre.

Fiction

Very young children need to become familiar with a bank of well-known stories, some of which need to be traditional tales. Children need to become familiar with story language and should be supported in retelling and sequencing well-known stories. Children should be introduced to texts with repetitive structures and predictable vocabulary, including stories with rhyming words. Story sacks provide a wonderful opportunity to tell and retell familiar stories, and children can be introduced to puppets to encourage them to engage in the retelling of a familiar text. You need to ensure that you create an attractive reading area where children can share books together or with adults or read alone. Story CDs are another useful resource to accompany books and support children in becoming familiar with stories. The reading area should contain books produced by the children as well as books scribed by you. Enlarged texts and digital texts also aid familiarisation. Washing-line activities enable children to sequence illustrations from stories, and children can also sequence text from stories. Children should have opportunities to re-enact stories through role play and drama. Classroom themes and areas of provision can be developed by using a carefully chosen text as an initial stimulus. You also need to consider how other areas of children's development, such as creative development, can be linked to a favourite book.

As children become familiar with texts, they should start to use book language in their spoken language. They will start to repeat words and phrases from well-loved stories and eventually they will transfer this language into their own writing. To become an independent writer, a child needs to merge several skills which may develop at different rates. These include phonic knowledge, compositional skills and transcription skills. You should also model being a reader and writer by reading stories alongside children and composing your own stories with them.

Once children are confident in retelling a range of familiar stories, they can start to create new stories of their own by making adaptations to an original story. This can be done in a range of ways including:

- changing the name of a character;
- changing the setting;
- substituting one event for a different event;
- changing the ending;
- changing the plot;
- introducing a new event;
- retelling the story from another character's point of view.

The advantage of this approach is that children can write adapted stories using the scaffold of the original story. You can challenge more able children by asking them to change more than one thing. Sometimes we ask young children to invent stories from scratch, when many of them do not have experiences of life, text and drama to support them in doing so. This process is a bridge between repeating well-known stories and inventing their own stories.

When children become confident in adapting stories and have sufficient experience of children's literature, they can begin to create their own stories. They need to be taught that stories follow a specific structure. All stories have a beginning, a build-up, a climax (problem), a resolution and an ending. Using shared texts you must point out these specific features of stories.

The process of writing a story needs to be addressed in stages and very carefully structured. Each stage needs to be modelled and opportunities should be given for children to apply this learning. You could easily spend a series of lessons teaching children about the features of story openers and another series of lessons teaching them about the features of a good character description. The point we are making here is that your teaching needs to be focused. You need to focus your lessons on different elements of a story and eventually children will put these together to write a complete story.

Developing children's abilities to write stories takes time. Very young children are capable of writing simple stories using a few sentences. As children progress and they begin to develop a wider range of knowledge and skills, their stories will demonstrate increasing complexity. You need to examine progression in terms of the quality of the writing rather than the quantity. Children can write an extensive story which is of very poor quality in terms of its content. While we agree that spelling, grammar and punctuation are important, stories also need to engage the reader. A story with perfect spelling and punctuation but lacking in ambitious vocabulary and interesting content does not necessarily do so. Equally children might use ambitious vocabulary and include imaginative content but spelling, handwriting and punctuation may impede the overall quality of the work. You therefore need to decide what focus you are looking for in the stories you ask your pupils to write. You cannot expect children to focus on too many skills at any one time. You need to communicate the intended focus and assess the outcomes against this.

Non-fiction

Children need to be introduced to the structural and language features of a range of non-fiction texts. In the early years and early primary phase these should include:

*   instructional texts;
*   recounts;
*   explanation texts;
*   discussion writing;
*   lists;
*   non-chronological reports;
*   simple persuasive writing.

You need to show children models of each of these text types in shared and guided reading and you need to structure your lessons carefully so that you introduce them to the specific features of each text type. Children also need opportunities to produce collaborative texts with you in shared writing and this will enable you to model the genre-specific features. Once you have researched these features, you need to plan meaningful lessons which provide a context for the writing that you ask children to produce. You could link the writing task into a broader theme. For example, if the children are studying a theme on 'Long Ago', they could write a simple non-chronological report on life in Victorian times. This will enable you to link the historical learning that children are undertaking with aspects of literacy. If the children have been learning about animals in science, they could produce a discussion text in literacy about the arguments for and against keeping animals in zoos. If the children have visited the local shopping precinct as part of a geography unit on the local environment, they could write a letter to the local council about the problem of litter or graffiti. Linking the learning in this way provides children with a more coherent curriculum and contexts and purposes for the writing.

Shared and guided writing

The purpose of shared writing is to enable you to model the writing process. Initially, young children need to see you modelling the process of writing simple captions and simple sentences. At this stage you can model skills such as segmentation, spacing, sentence structure and punctuation. As children become more advanced writers you can then start to model the genre-specific features and complex sentence structure.

We suggest a possible structure for a shared writing session below:

Teacher demonstration

- Share the key features that you are looking for in the writing with the children. For example, you might be focusing on the use of punctuation or the use of specific vocabulary such as adjectives, conjunctions or connectives.

- Firstly model the process of thinking before you write anything.

- Orally articulate your first caption or sentence and model the process of revising your initial thoughts. Thinking aloud helps to make the thought processes involved in writing more explicit.

- Record your first caption/sentence, drawing attention to the use of spacing between words, punctuation and making the segmentation process explicit.

Shared composition

- Ask the children to think of ideas for how the writing might develop. Give them thinking time and you could ask them to think in pairs. You could also give them mini-whiteboards to record their ideas.

- Ask them to share their ideas with you. Thank them for their ideas but don't write down the first idea because the ideas will often improve as the children's ideas are shared.

- Select the best idea and record it. Tell the children that all the ideas were good but you could not use all of them and they can use the other ideas in their own writing.

- Continue as above, asking the children to think of ideas, and keep selecting the best ideas for inclusion in the shared text.

- Read through the writing with the children and draw their attention to the features that you were focusing on.

- Model the process of editing the writing by crossing out words and adding new words to improve the writing.

As children become more confident writers they will start to plan their writing using a range of planning frameworks including story maps, story boards, flow charts, time lines and mind maps. We recommend that you model the process of how to do a plan because children may attempt to produce the whole finished product on the plan. You need to teach the children that the plan is just for recording key ideas and not for writing the finished product.

A unit of work on any genre should be structured through a range of lessons which culminate in producing an independent piece of writing. However, before children reach the stage of producing a finished recount, story, letter or poem they need to be taught the structural and language features of the genre, and shared writing gives you the opportunity to model these through composing a shared text which the children have ownership of. The children also need rich practical experiences to underpin their literacy work. For example, if they are going to write a recount it makes more sense if they have initially participated in a practical activity which provides a context for the final text.

Critical question

»   *In what ways might shared writing stifle children's creativity?*

Guided writing provides you with an opportunity to work with smaller groups of children. While shared writing is usually done with the whole class, guided writing is usually done with small groups of children organised on the basis of ability. The rationale for this approach is that grouping children by ability in writing enables you to focus on the specific knowledge, skills and understanding that the children need in order to further develop their writing. It may be that the children in the group are not demarcating sentences using capital letters and full stops, and guided writing enables you to focus on this particular aspect. Alternatively, you could have a group of children who are using punctuation really well but need to focus more on the use of descriptive vocabulary to provide the reader with more detail. Guided writing will enable you to provide groups of writers with really focused, specific input which will have a significant impact on their writing development.

Before you are able to plan for guided writing you will need to know your learners really well in terms of their development in writing. Just because a child may be a fluent reader, it does not automatically follow that their writing will be on a par. You also need to remember that children's development varies across subjects, so a really competent mathematician may be a poor writer. This has implications for the way you group children. Assuming that you have detailed knowledge about the progress of your learners in writing, you then need to know what to teach each group to move them forward. This is where a theoretical model or framework of writing development can come in useful, such as the one we mentioned at the beginning of this chapter. Additionally, many schools now use assessment criteria as a basis for future planning, so you could draw on these to support you in planning for future learning needs. We suggest a possible structure below to help you with planning guided writing sessions:

• Remind the group about the group writing target.

• Model some writing but maintain an explicit focus on the writing target.

• Provide the children with an opportunity to produce their own writing but emphasise that you want to see how well they address the focus writing target.

• Support the children as they compose their writing, encouraging them to think of their ideas first, speak their ideas out loud and share their ideas with a partner before writing them down.

• At the end of the lesson remind the children about the writing target and ask them to self-assess their own work or peer-assess the work of a partner with a focus on the writing target.

• Share one good piece of work produced by a child and tell them why it is good by drawing their attention to how well the child has addressed the writing target.

• Share 'next steps' with the group.

Guided writing provides a bridge between shared writing and independent writing. It needs to be built into the teaching sequence because it should enable the children to produce independent work of higher quality at the end of the unit. It is differentiated and focused and should help the children to progress in their writing. We recommend that it should not be a decontextualised activity, in that it should be meaningful and relate to other learning that children are undertaking in the classroom. It could relate to a topic or theme or it could relate to a shared text.

Critical questions

» *What are the advantages and disadvantages of grouping children by ability in writing?*

» *To what extent does guided writing limit children's creativity in writing?*

INTERNATIONAL PERSPECTIVES

In Denmark and Finland, children write much less at the age of six than their English counterparts. In those countries, there is a greater focus on oral language than there is in England. However, other countries outperform England in the international league tables. Could the focus in England on getting children to write, at the expense of oral development, be counter-productive?

Critical reflection

Writing is a hot potato, and politicians have expressed concerns for a number of years about children's under-achievement in writing.

»   *Why do you think boys' achievement in writing lags behind girls' achievement?*

»   *What strategies might accelerate boys' achievement?*

»   *Look through the expected levels of achievement in writing in both the Early Years Foundation Stage and Key Stage 1. Do you think that the expectations are appropriate?*

»   *To what extent do the curricula expectations in writing (such as the focus on spelling, grammar, punctuation, sentence structure and the features of different genres) limit children's creativity in writing?*

»   *Children are now digitally literate. Given the growth in use of computers and other hardware and software, how important is it to teach the skills of transcription?*

Critical points

This chapter has emphasised the importance of:

»   *valuing children's early attempts at writing;*

»   *teachers modelling the writing process;*

»   *motivating children by providing them with purposeful contexts for writing, drawing upon their own interests and providing children with a range of audiences for writing;*

»   *adopting a developmental approach by focusing on children's next steps in writing;*

»   *developing your own subject knowledge by researching into the structural and language features of each genre.*

Taking it further

Corbett, P. (2003) *How to Teach Story Writing at Key Stage 1*. London: David Fulton.

Latham, D. (2002) *How Children Learn to Write: Supporting and Developing Children's Writing in School*. London: Paul Chapman Publishing.

8 Early handwriting

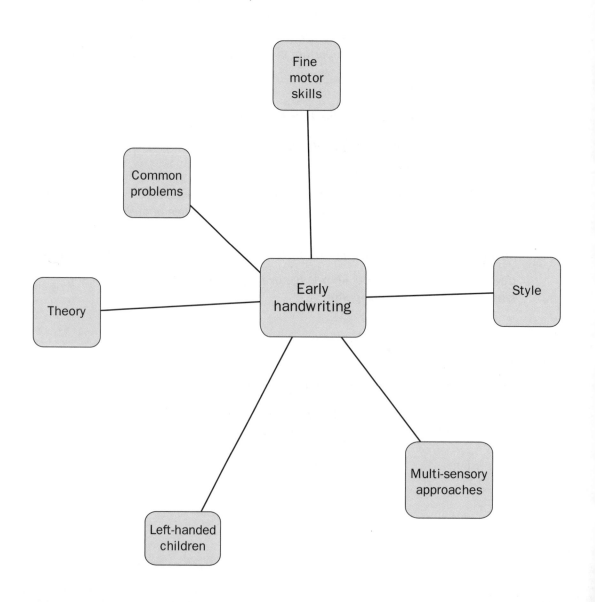

Links to the Early Years Foundation Stage

Physical development: Moving and handling

In the Development Matters statements of the Early Years Foundation Stage, emphasis is initially placed on the development of gross motor skills. Children are eventually expected to control a pencil, and by the end of the Early Years Foundation Stage children are expected to be able to form recognisable letters, most of which are correctly formed.

Links to the National Curriculum

By the end of Key Stage 1, children are expected to form letters correctly using correct proportions relative to one another. By the end of Key Stage 1 they are expected to use some of the joining strokes.

The theory

According to Brien (2012), *it has been accepted for some years that a joined style of writing (cursive) improves spelling because it encourages children to approach a whole word as a single complex movement.* However, this correlation has been disputed by some academics.

Fine motor skills

Children need to have good manipulative skills, hand/eye co-ordination and finger strength in order to succeed in handwriting.

Manipulative skills can be developed using a range of resources. Play-dough is a very useful resource for this purpose, and children can use it in a range of ways including squeezing, stretching, rolling and pressing. Finger puppets are another valuable resource to help children manipulate their fingers. Using finger puppets, children can separate their fingers wide apart, interlock their fingers, wiggle their fingers and thumb and open their fingers out from a fist one at a time.

Hand/eye co-ordination can be developed through:

- threading;
- using peg boards;
- weaving;
- using scissors;
- throwing and catching;
- hammering.

Finger/hand strength can be developed through:

- crushing paper;
- cutting thick card;

- squeezing a soft ball;
- digging;
- cutting food.

Unless these fine motor skills are developed first, children will find handwriting difficult because they will lack the foundations which are needed to control a writing implement.

Style

Broomfield and Combley (2003) argue that it is logical to link a grapheme with hand movements so that as the sound is introduced children then immediately practise the formation of the grapheme. This should be addressed through multi-sensory approaches. As children are presented with a range of texts they will also be presented with print in a range of scripts. There is debate regarding whether very young children should or should not be introduced to a cursive script. In cursive script, all letter formation begins at the bottom of the letter on a base line and the letters *f, g, j* and *y* have loops. The writing tool is rarely removed from the page whilst forming each letter, and each letter formation ends with an exit stroke. Letters are joined together from the exit stroke of the previous letter which moves into the approach stroke of the next letter. Broomfield and Combley (2003) argue that the cursive approach lessens the load on the memory because all letters start from the base line and the written word is completed without taking the writing implement off the page. For younger learners this approach can be problematic because the texts they are presented with will not reflect this writing style. Some teachers prefer semi-print styles, as adopted in schemes such as Marion Richardson and Nelson. The disadvantage of using a semi-print style is that children have to adapt their letter formation when they start to join their writing. Schools adopt handwriting schemes which form a whole-school handwriting policy. You should of course follow the policy adopted by your own school.

Brien (2012) identifies families of letters which are formed in specific ways. These include those that begin with anticlockwise movements including *a, c, d, f, g, o* and *q*. Some letters start with a down stroke including *l, h, b, I, k, j, t, r, m, n, p, u* and *y*. Other letters start with a slanting down stroke such as *w, x* and *v*. Three letters do not fit into these groupings: *e, s* and *z*. The formation of these letters can therefore be taught in groups which have similar starting points. We would advocate that you initially teach the formation of the graphemes, as the phonemes are taught within the suggested sequence of the daily Systematic Synthetic Phonics scheme. Once children have developed grapheme–phoneme correspondence for the entire alphabet, they will require further opportunities to consolidate their skills in letter formation. This is where we would advocate teaching the letter formation in letter groups. Brien (2012) also advocates introducing children to a handwriting style which separates the graphemes as units rather than linking them through the whole word. We consider this a logical approach given that children are learning grapheme–phoneme correspondence within a Systematic Synthetic Phonics programme. Linking graphemes throughout a word in a joined cursive script may impede children's recognition of the individual phonemes and graphemes.

Studies relating to the advantages of introducing a cursive script to young children have been inconclusive, although it is generally accepted that this may improve spelling as it encourages children to write a word as a single and continuous movement which is stored in the body. However, some maintain that Systematic Synthetic Phonics supports children in spelling words by segmenting them into their individual graphemes. Therefore Brien's approach would seem more logical because it reinforces segmentation.

Critical questions

»   *Do you think that children should learn to write using a cursive script or a print/ semi-print style? Explain your answer.*

»   *Do you agree that a handwriting style should reinforce graphemes as distinct units rather than linking graphemes through the whole word?*

Multi-sensory approaches

Children initially must master the hand movements necessary to form each letter. Initially these may be gross motor movements, and with practice children should then be encouraged to refine these same movements. When teaching letter formation the following steps will support you.

•   *Look*: the teacher models the formation of a large letter on the board. Interactive whiteboards are not ideal for this purpose as the alignment is often inaccurate.

•   *Trace*: the child traces over the letter repeatedly while also articulating the sound. Avoid tracing over dotted letters, as children may focus on joining the dots and this will impede the flow of the letter formation.

•   *Copy*: the child copies the letter repeatedly while also articulating the sound.

•   *Write from memory*: the model is removed and the child practises the formation of the letter.

•   *Eyes shut*: the child writes the letter from memory with their eyes shut to commit the letter formation to memory.

Letter formation should be practised using a variety of materials, including tracing in salt, sand and glitter, writing in the air, writing on each other's backs, tracing on hessian and silk or writing with water. It may be necessary to manipulate the child's hand to support letter formation. Initially the focus is on the child developing the correct movement for forming each letter. As the child progresses they can be introduced to tram lines which will help them to focus on proportion, ascenders and descenders.

Critical questions

»   *When should children be introduced to writing in pen?*

»   *How important is handwriting practice?*

»   *How can teachers monitor letter formation?*

»   *When children are writing freely would you continue to insist upon correct letter formation? How would you support your argument?*

Left-handed children

Many problems that left-handed children encounter can be solved in the following ways.

- Some younger left-handed children write from right to left, so a coloured dot next to the left-hand margin will remind them where to start.
- Pencil grips may aid pencil control.
- The child should hold the pencil at least 2cm away from the tip to make it easier for them to see what they are writing.
- Seat a left-handed child next to another left-handed child to avoid elbow clashing, or seat them to the left side of a right-handed child.
- Make allowances for smudging or allow them to slant their paper for writing.
- Provide a slope for writing.

Common problems

Handwriting can be painful and children often get into bad habits by forming letters incorrectly. You will need to monitor the way that children form their letters, and not just the final presentation. We recommend that handwriting is taught in small groups so that the teacher can observe the children's letter formation very carefully. You will also need to make sure that your own letter formation follows the format of the handwriting scheme that is being used in the school. You will need to pay very careful attention to the way in which you model letter formation, and in particular you will need to ensure that you start the letter in the correct place.

CREATIVE APPROACH

You must not be tempted to thrust a pencil into a child's hand and work tirelessly to develop their handwriting. Before the development of fine motor skills which facilitate the control of a pencil, children will require extensive opportunities to practise and develop their gross motor skills. It is only when gross motor skills are strong that children will be ready to develop the precision required to use a pencil effectively. Children can practise gross motor movements using ribbon sticks, responding to music by making large movements and small movements. Additionally, children can make large or small movements in response to music using finger paints. If the music is jerky they can make spiky movements, if it is quiet they can make smooth, flowing movements and if it is fast they can make fast movements. Later in their development, children can practise forming recognisable letters and shapes using wet sand, chunky chalks, wet cornflour, glitter and gloop.

CASE STUDY

Toheed started a new school at the beginning of Year 2. His parents immediately sought help and advice in relation to his handwriting which was under-developed. They explained that he had had daily practice in his previous school to improve his handwriting, in the form of formal handwriting sessions. They had also purchased additional materials to enable him to practise at home. Such interventions had had little impact on Toheed's handwriting. A multi-sensory approach was introduced to Toheed. He was engaged in short, daily sessions, the focus of which was to develop his gross motor skills. Moving his arms to music supported him in further developing his gross motor skills. Responding to music was particularly beneficial as it enabled him to practise a wide range of movements. He responded to the music with paint, ribbon sticks and making marks in dry and wet sand. Once his gross motor skills were established, Toheed followed a programme to develop his fine motor skills. This included activities such as threading, picking up objects with tweezers or pegs and mark-making in paint and wet sand with finer tools.

- Why did the school not continue with the handwriting programme that had been established in Toheed's previous school?

Critical questions

» *How important is handwriting in society today given the growth of computer-generated text?*

» *How important is it for children to write neatly?*

Critical reflection

In society, adults tend to handwrite for informal purposes, such as making quick notes and lists. For situations when neater presentation is required we tend to use word-processing packages to produce finished pieces of writing. Taking this into consideration, how important do you think it is for children to develop a neat handwriting style? Additionally, the focus on handwriting can sometimes restrict children's creativity. Is it more important for children to write creatively or to write neatly?

Critical points

This chapter has emphasised the importance of:

» *adopting a multi-sensory approach to handwriting;*

» *developing gross motor skills before the development of fine motor skills.*

Taking it further

Medwell, J. and Wray, D. (2008) Handwriting – A Forgotten Language Skill? *Language and Education*, 22, (1): 34–47.

9 Early spelling

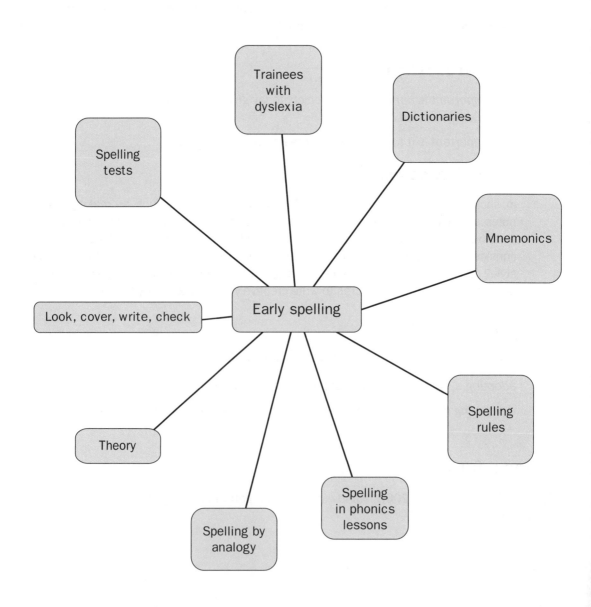

Links to the Early Years Foundation Stage

Literacy: Writing

The Early Years Foundation Stage emphasises that children should be able to use their phonic knowledge to spell words which match their spoken sounds. Additionally, they should be able to write some common irregular words by the end of the Early Years Foundation Stage.

Links to the National Curriculum

The National Curriculum emphasises the need for children to use their phonic knowledge to write phonetically regular words. Additionally it emphasises the need for children to spell specifically identified words correctly.

The theory

Henderson (1985) has established a theory of development which suggests that children move through a sequence of phases as they develop their skills in spelling. Initially children's development in spelling is pre-phonetic and is characterised by simple mark-making. Children then progress through a semi-phonetic phase where they represent some of the sounds within words with the corresponding graphemes. Children progress to the phonetic stage where simple consonant–vowel–consonant words are written correctly but they do not yet understand all the spelling patterns. During the more advanced stages of spelling development in this model, children start to develop an understanding of larger units of sound within words as well as an understanding of prefixes and suffixes and the ability to apply more complex spelling rules.

Spelling in phonics lessons

In the daily phonics lesson, you will teach children to spell words by listening to each phoneme in sequence and articulating the phonemes (oral segmentation) and by writing the graphemes that correspond with the phonemes. You should be teaching children that blending and segmenting are reversible processes. However, you will find that children do not automatically transfer this skill into their independent writing. You should therefore encourage children to make an attempt at spellings by listening to the phonemes in the words they are attempting to write and you should accept, value and praise their phonetically plausible attempts at spelling words.

The problem with using phonics for spelling is that it only works if the words are phonetically regular (d-o-g/g-oa-t). However, children will also apply this strategy to irregular words. In our view this is absolutely fine because it demonstrates that children are making an attempt at a word and are working independently. There is nothing worse than queues of children waiting for the teacher to provide spellings, and this creates a dependency culture. Children should be encouraged to have a go at spelling words, and the main strategy they will draw on is their knowledge of the sounds in the word.

Your feedback on children's attempts at spellings needs to take into account the level of the alphabetic code they have reached. You may have taught 'oa', but it will not prevent children from writing 'rowd' instead of 'road'. In this instance you should point out that although 'ow' and 'oa' can make the same sound, the correct grapheme to use in this instance is 'oa'. However, if children have written 'rowd' but not yet been introduced to 'oa' then it is probably not worth pointing out.

As part of their Systematic Synthetic Phonics lessons children will be introduced to 'tricky' words such as *said* and *the* and you will specifically draw their attention to the tricky part of the word. However, having taught *said* in a phonics lesson, if you notice a child has written 's-e-d' in their independent work you might want to draw their attention to this by highlighting the error and reminding them about the tricky part of the word. However if they have written 's-e-d' and they have not yet been introduced to *said* then we recommend that you praise them for their attempt rather than drawing their attention to the error. In this way you can take account of the children's stage of development when you provide feedback. There is nothing worse than a child labouring over a piece of writing only for a teacher to destroy their work with spelling corrections.

Critical questions

» *Do you agree that children's attempts at spellings should be valued?*

» *Should all spelling mistakes be corrected?*

» *Should teachers model incorrect spellings on the board?*

Look, cover, write, check

This approach relies on a strong visual memory. The process is as follows.

Look: children look at the word carefully, memorise it and say it.

Cover: children cover the word.

Write: children write the word from memory.

Check: children check their spelling attempt against the word.

Critical questions

» *What are the advantages and disadvantages of this approach?*

» *What problems might this method create if schools are using Systematic Synthetic Phonics?*

Spelling by analogy

Spelling by analogy is a useful strategy and enables children to realise that words can be grouped. If they can spell *coat* then they can probably spell *goat*, *boat* and *throat* (providing they know 'th-r'). However, the strategy does not work for all words. For example, knowing how to spell *goat* will not help with the spelling of *note*. Drawing children's attention to the rime can be useful some of the time and consequently this strategy is worthy of consideration.

Mnemonics

These provide a way of remembering tricky words such as:

- *necessary* – one collar and two sleeves;
- *because* – big elephants can always understand small elephants;
- *separate* – there is *a rat* in 'sep*ara*te';
- *said* – Sally-Anne is dancing.

Critical questions

» *What are the advantages and disadvantages of spelling by analogy?*

» *What are the advantages and disadvantages of using mnemonics?*

Spelling rules

You will remember spelling rules that you were taught at school. A common rule that everyone knows is *i before e except after c*. Rules are useful but the main problem with rules is that there are always exceptions because the English language is so irregular. Teaching children spelling rules is appropriate once they are able to decode words for reading. In this way the focus tends to shift from reading to spelling. Many children with dyslexia do eventually master learning to read, but spelling can remain a lifelong problem for them. Additionally, many non-dyslexics also struggle with spelling. Some people seem to be better at spelling than others, but by learning a few simple rules most people can become better at spelling. Spelling is important because society is quick to make judgements about people who make spelling errors. However, as teachers we do not want children to avoid using interesting words just because they cannot spell them. We would rather children make a really good attempt at writing *delicious* than use the word *nice*. When you mark children's work you need to be sensitive about their spelling errors and it is certainly not appropriate to correct them all. This will destroy children's self-concepts. What you can do is focus on those spellings or spelling rules that you know the children have been taught and use it as an opportunity to reinforce the rule. Additionally, try to focus on common spelling errors that children keep repeating.

Brien (2012) provides an overview of some useful spelling rules. These include:

- Add 'es' to make a plural when the plural adds a syllable, as in *class/classes*.
- 'Q' is followed by 'u' and another vowel.
- Words do not end in 'j' or 'v'.
- If a word ends in a vowel you drop it before adding a suffix, as in *make/making*.
- Prefixes never alter the root word, for example *do/undo*; *zip/unzip*.

There are of course exceptions to these rules and there are other rules too. You will need to research the rule. A few years ago the National Strategies produced a very comprehensive document which went through all the key spelling rules. It was entitled *Support for Spelling*. Although the organisation has now ceased to exist it will be enormously beneficial if you can locate a copy of this document.

You need to teach the spelling rules explicitly and we recommend the following approach.

Revisit: revisit specific spelling rules that children have previously been taught, for example by focusing on those rules which the pupils find tricky.

Teach: introduce the new rule by modelling how the rule works. You might want to show how the rule is applied to two or three words.

Practise: give the children time to investigate the spelling rule, perhaps by organising them into pairs and asking them to apply the rule to other words. You might want them to find exceptions to the rule.

Apply: give the children a sentence to write which requires them to apply the rule.

You need to bear in mind that just because children have been taught a rule does not mean that they will automatically apply that rule in their own independent writing. Children may be able to apply the rule within the spelling lesson but they may forget the rule when it comes to their own writing. If the children have been taught a rule, you should make a specific point about this when you provide them with feedback, perhaps by reminding them of the rule and then giving them further opportunities to apply it.

Dictionaries

Dictionaries are a useful resource to support children with their independent writing. They can use them to locate spellings of words or definitions and this will reduce the pressure on you by breaking their dependency on you to provide the spellings.

We recommend starting with simple picture dictionaries because the picture cue helps children to locate the word. As children progress they will need to be taught explicitly how dictionaries work because the dictionaries become more complex. You will need to teach them how to locate words in a dictionary using their knowledge of alphabetic ordering. Initially this can be taught by teaching them how to locate words using the first letter only. More able children can progress on to ordering words by the second and third letters, so you can give them words beginning with the same initial letter but with different subsequent letters and you can ask them to put the words in order. Children need experience of ordering words firstly by the first letter, then the second and third letters and so on. They also need experience of locating words in dictionaries. They need to be taught these skills in the daily literacy lesson and then they need opportunities to apply these skills when writing independently. The transference of this skill may not be automatic, so the skill of using dictionaries may need to be further reinforced in guided reading sessions. Children should also be taught how to use electronic dictionaries and simple electronic spell checkers. Alphabet mats on tables to show alphabetic order are also a useful resource.

Trainees with dyslexia

The first point we wish to make is that we have trained many trainees with dyslexia and they have made excellent teachers. Dyslexia should not prevent you from progressing successfully through your course, and just because you have dyslexia does not mean that you will make a bad teacher. Indeed, we have found that personal experiences of dyslexia may make you a more effective teacher, but the situation needs careful thought because of your role as an educator.

Crucially, in order to pass your placement you will need to demonstrate that you have good subject knowledge. Therefore, making spelling mistakes and reading errors in front of children is unlikely to help you in demonstrating that you have achieved the following Teachers' Standards (DFE, 2012):

- *be accountable for pupils' attainment, progress and outcomes*

- *demonstrate an understanding of and take responsibility for promoting high standards of literacy, articulacy and the correct use of standard English, whatever the teacher's specialist subject*

- *if teaching early reading, demonstrate a clear understanding of Systematic Synthetic Phonics.*

As a teacher you are expected to promote high standards of literacy, and as a primary school teacher you play a critical role in ensuring that your children can read and write. The standards agenda which pervades education demands high standards of pupil achievement in reading and writing. Pupil achievement is high on the agenda, and so in order for your pupils to reach high standards in reading and writing you need to ensure that you can model the skills and knowledge necessary for them to achieve.

However, if you have an official diagnosis of dyslexia then you are protected by the Equality Act (2010) which means that all educational institutions have a responsibility for making reasonable adjustments to enable you to reach your potential. This is because as well as being a trainee teacher you are also a learner and you may be attending a higher education institution which must comply with the equality legislation. Additionally, when you are working in school, either during a placement or through an employment-based initial teacher training route, the school has a responsibility to make reasonable adjustments to enable you to reach your full potential.

Consequently, your training provider and the school should work together and jointly plan the reasonable adjustment that you need to support you with reading and writing. You may only need a few simple adjustments to help you to succeed through your training. These might include:

- access to a laptop computer;

- access to a computer spell checker or computer dictionaries;

- access to a dictaphone to record important points that you need to action from meetings with your mentor or tutor;

- access to software to help you with planning and structuring assignments and reports;

- access to a supportive tutor who will check your spellings for you.

The nature of the specific adjustments you require will depend on your specific needs. You should feel confident about declaring your dyslexia to your training provider and your schools because legally they have a duty to support you to achieve your full educational potential. They are not allowed to discriminate against you directly or indirectly because of your dyslexia.

We have found that trainees with dyslexia provide very effective role models for pupils with learning difficulties. They understand their difficulties and they make caring and empathic teachers. This is supported by Burns and Bell (2010; 2011). Additionally, they know how to break learning down into more achievable steps so that their learners can make progress. In this way they become skilled at differentiating tasks. This is supported by Griffiths (2012).

We support a social model of disability which assumes that disability is a socially constructed phenomenon rather than something which is located within a person's biological make-up. In supporting this model we choose to differentiate between impairment and disability as two fundamentally different concepts. Thus, you may have an impairment (dyslexia) which is part of your biological make-up but this should not prevent you from achieving your potential, providing that appropriate provision has been put in place to help you. If you are prevented from achieving your potential because institutions have not made reasonable adjustments then you can be said to have been disabled. In this sense, disability becomes a social construct. Our view is that you should be honest about your dyslexia to your provider or schools, because this will enable them to provide adjustments to help you. If you do not tell them about it then they cannot be held to account and you may not achieve your potential.

However, we do not think that you should use dyslexia as an excuse for poor teaching. As an educator you are accountable for the education of your pupils. You might find spelling difficult but we would expect you to be proactive in getting the support you require and, as you will be aware from your own experiences of school, you may simply need to work harder to prepare for your lessons in advance. We recommend that you work collaboratively with your provider and the school in planning the additional support that you require. You should be involved in this process and this will maximise your chances of success. However, this does not always mean that things will run smoothly. No one can prepare you for the words that children will throw at you when they ask for spellings or in shared writing lessons when you have to record their ideas. It might be better to acknowledge your weaknesses to the children. You could tell them that you find spelling tricky and that you need to look up the word. This is a useful strategy because it demonstrates to pupils that you are not perfect, that you are a learner and that it is acceptable not to know something. If you have an electronic spell checker handy, you could type that word into the spell checker and you will then know how to spell the word. You could model how to look up words in dictionaries or typing the spelling into a Word document and right clicking on it to find the correct spelling. These strategies are useful because they enable you to model the skills that independent writers need. Also, children are unlikely to disrespect you if you are honest with them, but they are more likely to do so if you pretend that you are perfect.

Access to a supportive school and supportive mentor are vital. In relation to trainees with dyslexia it has been argued that *they are often seen as threats to standards and a burden, requiring extra work rather than a valuable resource to promote understanding and acceptance of disability in schools.*

(Griffiths, 2012, p 55)

Griffiths (2012) found that negative mentor feedback can impact on trainee teachers' self-concepts. Additionally, in a society which prizes perfection, trainees with dyslexia are sometimes seen as a threat to high standards (Riddick, 2001; 2003). We find this worrying, given that we have trained so many outstanding, creative and inspirational trainees with dyslexia.

Critical questions

» *How important is correct spelling in children's writing?*

» *Do you think the quality of children's ideas is more important than the quality of their spelling?*

» *Do you think that we live in a society that prizes perfection (Griffiths, 2012)?*

Spelling tests

Many schools and teachers use weekly spelling tests to monitor pupils' progress in spelling. We do not support this model of teaching spelling, because spelling tests can damage children's self-concepts, particularly those of pupils who receive low marks on a consistent basis. Additionally, children do not automatically transfer this learning to their independent writing. A correct spelling in a spelling test does not mean that this word will be spelt correctly in pupils' independent writing.

We prefer a model where teachers focus more on children's spelling in their independent writing. If a spelling has been taught and then the word is spelt incorrectly in a piece of independent writing this could become a focus for the feedback and teachers can subsequently monitor children's progress in spelling this word. Although teachers attempt to differentiate spelling tests by giving different spellings to different groups of learners, spelling is a very individual skill. Therefore it is more appropriate to select two or three spellings for children to focus on individually and then to monitor their progress in spelling these words. When they have mastered the spellings and are applying the skill in their independent writing, you can give them two or three more spellings to focus on. The lists of spellings for specific year groups in the new draft National Curriculum are useful, albeit challenging, but we would advise teachers to focus on these with individual children rather than implementing spelling tests with whole classes or groups. There seems little point in giving children a new spelling list each week if there are still errors from the previous week that show that the child has not mastered specific words. Obviously our approach has staffing implications and you will not have the time to work on an individual basis with individual children on their spelling each week. However, if you are working with young children they should have weekly reading conferences with an adult. This would be a good opportunity to monitor their progress in spelling by checking that they can read and write the words that you have given them to practise. In this way you can share the load with your teaching assistant(s). Giving them only a small handful of words to focus on will make the process more manageable for you and them, but you will need to keep making sure that they are spelling the words correctly in their independent writing. You will also need to periodically revisit specific words to check that they have retained the spellings.

Critical question

» *What are the arguments for and against spelling tests?*

CREATIVE APPROACH

Brien (2012) recommends creating a spelling area in the classroom which includes:

- word lists;
- spelling rules;
- dictionaries;
- thesauruses;
- electronic spell checkers;
- theme/ topic words.

We agree with this and wish to emphasise the importance of creating a print-rich environment to support children's independence in spelling. Your classroom could include all of the above as well as additional material such as tricky-word walls, word banks, word mats, alphabet mats and electronic aids to support spelling.

Where possible we recommend that children practise writing words using multi-sensory approaches including:

- writing in glitter, sand, salt;
- writing in the air;
- writing words with chunky chalks.

CASE STUDY

Aba was a trainee in a Year 2 class. She was aware that from time to time she found spelling difficult. Aba chose to approach this difficulty positively. On the occasions when she was unsure of the spelling of a word she informed the children of this and she modelled to them the ways in which spellings could be checked. This included the use of dictionaries and spell checkers on computers.

Critical questions

» *Do you think that it was acceptable for Aba to share her weaknesses in spelling with the children?*

» *How did Aba turn her weak spelling skills into a tool for teaching?*

Critical reflection

The new draft National Curriculum identifies spellings that children must master each year before progressing into the next year. Some of these words include spellings that are quite challenging.

» *What effect do you think this will have on children's attitudes towards spelling?*

» *Do you agree that it is necessary to 'raise the bar' in this way?*

» *Do you think that society places too much emphasis on spelling?*

Critical points

This chapter has emphasised the importance of:

» *monitoring children's application of spelling from taught sessions which focus on spelling to their independent writing;*

» *ensuring feedback takes account of the spellings and spelling rules that children have been taught;*

» *teaching spellings on an individual basis and monitoring individual achievement rather than through the implementation of whole-class spelling tests;*

» *being honest with pupils, mentors and training providers about your own difficulties (if any) with spelling;*

» *creating a print-rich environment which facilitates the development of spelling.*

Taking it further

O'Sullivan, O. and Thomas, A. (2007) *Understanding Spelling.* London: The Centre for Literacy in Primary Education.

10 Early literacy through the wider learning environment

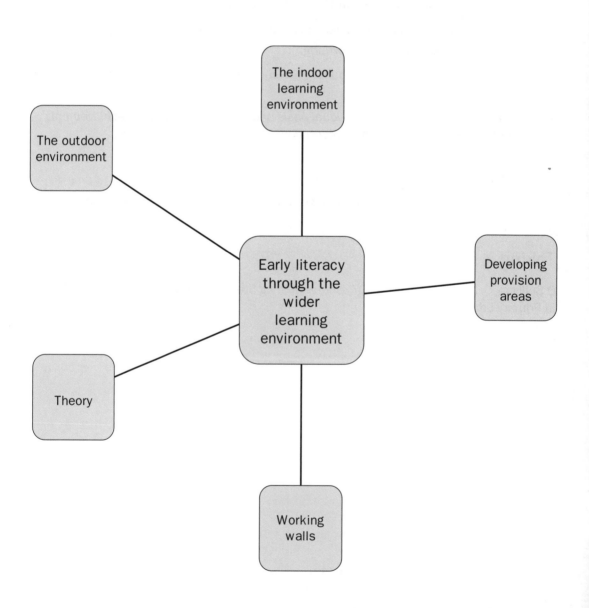

Links to the Early Years Foundation Stage

Communication and language: Listening and attention

The Early Years Foundation Stage states that children need to *listen attentively in a range of situations*. This has implications for your enabling learning environment which should provide opportunities for children to listen to stories, rhymes and sounds as well as listening to adults.

Communication and language: Understanding

The Early Years Foundation Stage states that children need to listen and respond to ideas expressed by others. This has implications for your enabling learning environment which must be set up to facilitate the development of communication between children and between children and adults.

Communication and language: Speaking

The Early Years Foundation Stage emphasises that children must be able to talk for a wide range of purposes. This has implications for your enabling learning environment, which must facilitate talk, and you must value children's talk.

Literacy: Reading and writing

The Early Years Foundation Stage states that children need to use their phonic knowledge to decode and segment regular words and read and write common irregular words.

Links to the National Curriculum

The National Curriculum emphasises the inter-relationship between reading, writing, speaking and listening. Your learning environment should therefore give equal emphasis to all these strands of English.

The theory

The Rose Review (Rose, 2006) argues strongly that phonics work should be embedded within a broad and a rich language curriculum. This should include:

- opportunities for purposeful discussion;
- immersing children in the power of play, songs, rhymes and drama;
- developing children's vocabulary through adult–child interactions;
- a focus on reading, writing, speaking and listening.

To understand texts, children need to have a secure understanding of vocabulary. Muter et al. (2004) found that early vocabulary knowledge was a predictor of subsequent success in reading comprehension. Providing children with rich opportunities for talk and vocabulary development will enhance children's reading comprehension skills.

The indoor learning environment

Children's literacy and language development can be supported effectively through a well-planned learning environment which provides opportunities for reading, writing and speaking and listening. All of these aspects of literacy are inter-related and depend upon each other. Children do not just learn literacy in the daily literacy lesson. A language-rich environment serves several functions. Firstly it reinforces learning that children have been introduced to in taught lessons. Secondly it ensures that children are immersed in opportunities to read, write, speak and listen. Additionally it enables children to apply their knowledge, skills and understanding, both independently and with the support of their peers and adults.

Labels and captions support the development of children's reading skills. Resources and working areas should be clearly labelled, and for younger children the label should be accompanied by a picture cue. This facilitates independence and supports children in accessing resources independently. Children should be introduced to both word-processed and handwritten texts and these should be displayed at the child's eye level. Classroom displays should be accompanied by labels and captions which promote interaction. You will discover that children do not naturally engage with text around the room and you should draw their attention to the text. It is very important that children see adults producing texts and they must see them doing so in a variety of ways and for a variety of purposes. Children should also be encouraged to produce their own labels and captions which should be displayed and valued.

It is important that children's names are displayed in the classroom and that they have purposeful opportunities to write their names. Suggestions include asking children to self-register as well as asking them to write name labels to accompany their work on displays.

Days of the week and months of the year should also be clearly visible to children, as should greetings in a range of different languages; colour words; and numbers as words. Pictorial alphabet friezes and previously taught graphemes and tricky words should also be displayed in the environment. Children's own writing should also be clearly evident to communicate the value that is placed on their work. A range of text types should be displayed in the classroom, including captions, fiction, non-fiction and poetry.

It is very important that children see adults reading and writing for different purposes. Sometimes children benefit from observing their teacher reading or writing alongside them. You may have asked the children to create a poster or write a story and this is an activity that you can also participate in. As you work alongside the children you can share your ideas with them, allowing them to contribute to these, and you can share your final compositions. This ensures that the children begin to see you as an author as well as a learner. It is important that you model the process of editing your own work. Authors rarely produce a perfect draft, and children need to understand that it is acceptable and beneficial to make adaptations to their work to enhance it. You should scaffold learning by writing alongside children as they engage in independent play in areas of provision.

Signs which communicate information are important and should be an integral feature of an effective classroom. This is referred to as *functional print*. Examples include:

- classroom rules;

- daily schedules;

- group lists;

- a list of classroom helpers.

Word banks are a powerful way of developing children's independence in writing. We recommend that you focus on presenting familiar tricky words only, because children should be encouraged to use their phonic knowledge to segment words whenever possible. During the composition process, children can be encouraged to find words that they are unable to spell using alphabetic word banks, word walls or simple dictionaries. You may wish to engage children in adding words to these classroom resources.

There is no greater motivator for children than seeing their work valued and displayed in their classroom. Work can be included in displays, class books as well as published on the school intranet. Books produced by individual and groups of children should be included in class reading areas and school libraries. Writing in relation to all areas of the curriculum should be evident.

As part of a broad and rich language curriculum you should plan regular sessions in which you can share stories, poems and non-fiction texts to develop a love of literature. You need to ensure that you have researched into a range of stories which meet the needs and interests of different ages and abilities. You also need to be familiar with children's authors and different versions of stories. This subject knowledge is fundamental to your development as a teacher of young children. You should also develop the confidence to be able to tell stories to children so that you immerse them in imaginary worlds in a powerful and exciting way. Although shared reading is important, it cannot replace story time and story-telling. In shared reading sessions it is not always possible to read a complete text to children, whereas in story time and story-telling sessions it is possible to hear and share complete texts. Children should be familiar with simple rhymes, songs and poems and they should learn these by heart. As a teacher you should demonstrate a passion for stories, poems and non-fiction texts. It is not acceptable to communicate to children your personal preferences and thereby your dislike of some genre. Neither is it acceptable to avoid sharing different genres with children. You should try to write your own stories and poems as well as non-fiction texts and share these with the children. Explain that you are the author. They may wish to take your lead and produce similar texts of their own.

Books are also an effective stimulus for learning in other areas of the curriculum. For example you may wish to consider how the story of *Goldilocks and the Three Bears* could be used in mathematics to develop children's understanding of number and size. The same story could be used to create simple maps of the journey taken by the characters. Additionally the story of *The Three Little Pigs* could be used as an effective stimulus to explore materials.

Developing provision areas

Opportunities for children to read, write and communicate should be embedded across all areas in the classroom and not confined to a nominated writing area.

A book area can be created quite easily and is an essential development in all classrooms. It is important to include texts which relate to the current topic or theme that the children are learning about. You should always ensure that the children have access to a range of fiction, non-fiction, rhyming and poetry texts. The area should include comfortable seating and should be located in a quiet part of the classroom. You should encourage children to read individually as well as with their peers and adults. Even for very young children, the area should be designed with simple systems in mind to ensure that books can be located by the children. Baskets are an effective way of storing texts. The area should also be clearly labelled. You should plan opportunities for children to access this area independently as well as during guided and shared work. You should ensure that you provide some books with a repetitive structure as well as those that are completely decodable and some which focus on the tricky words that the children in your class have been taught.

A phonics area is a very valuable resource and offers children opportunities to practise and consolidate prior learning. You should carefully consider introducing a range of resources to the children to ensure that they remain motivated. These could include:

- whiteboards;
- letter fans;
- magnetic letters;
- chalk boards;
- alphabet bean bags;
- alphabet floor tiles;
- computer programs;
- glitter trays;
- sand trays;
- glitter pens.

Do not present all the resources at once. Changing and adding resources is a far more successful approach and will ensure that children remain engaged and motivated.

There should also be an appealing writing/mark-making area that includes a range of writing materials and papers, whiteboards, chalk boards and any other resources that excite and stimulate your children to write. This area should be enhanced to link with current learning themes as well as the children's interests. Children should be encouraged to access this area for both structured writing tasks and independent writing, and their attempts should be valued. The area should also include tricky words, graphemes and topic words.

You should also develop an inviting listening area which includes headphones, CDs and texts which cover all genres. Again these should link to current learning themes.

Opportunities for reading and writing in role play should be carefully planned as this area provides a perfect opportunity to engage children in writing for clear and specific purposes. Examples of these include writing shopping lists, telephone messages, prescriptions, food orders, Christmas gift lists and cards. You should ensure that there are planned opportunities for children to work alongside adults to enable you to model different purposes for writing. Reading opportunities should also be available in the role-play area as should puppets and small world equipment. This facilitates the development of language and communication.

Curiosity areas can be enhanced by including text. This could include, for example, texts relating to animals, interesting objects and materials. Resources to enable children to record their observations should also be available in the area.

In developing a malleable area, consider incorporating vocabulary that reflects learning in the area. For example, words such as *push, pull, roll, squash, pinch* and *stretch* could be displayed in this area. Children may also wish to draw or label their products, so you should ensure that resources which enable them to do so are readily available. You also need to plan opportunities for developing children's reading and writing skills in the sand and water areas. Adult-led literacy activities could be planned in these areas so that children can develop their reading and writing skills. Additionally, these resources could be enhanced by including resources such as graphemes or high-frequency words and the children could be left to play independently in these areas.

Children must be able to access a range of information and communication technology (ICT) hardware and software, including reading and writing software and interactive computer programs. We wish to emphasise that ICT is more than just computers and you should plan to include the use of programmable toys, listening centres, electronic mats, microphones and similar resources to develop children's reading, writing, speaking and listening skills. Some children who are reluctant to read and write with more conventional tools can be motivated to do so through the use of ICT resources.

All areas of classroom provision enable children to develop their vocabulary and communication. Children should be encouraged to communicate with each other, and adults can scaffold children's learning by working alongside children and extending their language development. Introducing children to new spoken and written vocabulary during their play will pave the way for subsequent success in reading.

You should ensure that your classroom resources reflect the diverse society in which children live. Children should have the opportunity to use multicultural resources and be exposed to images that display disability, different ethnicities and cultures.

Working walls

A working wall for literacy is an organic learning resource which supports children's learning in literacy. You can add information to the wall during a topic or unit of work so that the wall includes information relating to the text type(s) that children are studying. It is a unique type of display, in that it is not intended to be neat and tidy, and you should encourage the children to contribute to the development of the wall. We recommend that your working wall should include the following features, although this is not an exhaustive list:

- good models of the text type on which you are focusing. These should clearly show the structural features of the text type and pertinent vocabulary. They can be annotated to draw children's attention to these;

- genre checklists to remind the children about the structural and language features of the genre that the children are currently focusing on;

- mind maps to show the development of children's initial ideas relating to the identified text type;

- planning frameworks to support children in planning their writing and samples of children's plans;

- drafting – examples of shared writing composed by the class during the unit of work and drafts produced by children;

- key vocabulary that children need to use;

- samples of marked writing;

- WAGOLLs – *What A Good One Looks Like*: samples of the text type which clearly model your expectations. These may be samples produced by the children or may be models provided by you.

We recommend that schools develop a policy for the presentation of working walls to ensure that children are familiar with accessing them effectively. This will promote consistency across classes, and children will become secure as to how they are used and accessed. Familiarity will develop children's confidence in using the working walls.

The outdoor environment

The outdoor area should include opportunities for reading, writing, speaking, listening and communication. An effective way of facilitating communication is to use the outdoors for den making. Dens can also be built indoors, but the additional space afforded by the outdoors is genuinely more conducive to den building. Children can build their own dens and will often communicate more freely with their peers in these 'secret' and safe environments.

Reading and writing activities in the outdoors can be provided through adult-led or child-initiated independent play activities. The great advantage of the outdoors over the indoor environment is the space it often provides. Children can work on large sheets of paper and outdoor floor surfaces using chalks, paints and water for mark-making without inhibition. This enables them to develop their gross and fine motor skills which support the development of transcription skills. They can engage in activities similar to those in the indoor environment which offer rich learning experiences. The advantages of being outdoors are that activities can be bigger, noisier and the outdoor area offers greater opportunities for movement. Resources and activities which may be more accessible in the outdoor area could include:

- engaging children in actions linked to stories and rhymes;

- playing traditional games, for example 'What time is it Mr Wolf?';

- encouraging children to explore their voices by whispering and shouting;

- a book area within a shelter;

- large-scale mark-making opportunities which could include water, paint, chunky chalk or wet sand.

Critical questions

» *How beneficial is it for children to trace letters in the air, in glitter, in sand and to use chunky chalks to develop their transcription skills, when they will ultimately be required to write with a pencil?*

» *Do you think these gross motor skills ultimately help children with using a pencil?*

» *Would it not be better to focus on teaching children how to write with a pencil right from the start?*

Interaction with peers and adults is as necessary in the outdoor environment as in the indoor environment. You should be wary of dominating children's outdoor play. Your enthusiasm for play will however be welcomed by the children. The outdoors offers a wonderful opportunity to be creative and to develop literacy skills in what should be a very different environment. You should guard against creating a mirror image of the indoor environment as you develop the outdoors. It must be different and provide a space for activities that cannot be delivered indoors.

Critical questions

» *We have stressed that the outdoors should be used to provide activities which would be difficult to implement indoors. The outdoors provides you with an opportunity to work with children on a larger scale. Do you agree with the view that if an activity can be carried out indoors it should not be carried out outdoors?*

» *How can teachers mediate the tensions between providing an exciting, rich, stimulating range of activities and at the same time addressing the imperatives of the standards agenda, which demands that children produce neat, tidy and well-presented writing?*

CREATIVE APPROACH

The areas of provision in the classroom should provide children with opportunities to write in a range of media including:

- writing in glitter;

- writing in gloop;

- writing in shaving foam;

- writing in paint;

- writing in coloured sand using assorted colours;
- writing in jelly.

Hiding graphemes and words in sand and water is a valuable way of using these areas for teaching or reinforcing literacy.

CASE STUDY

Hayley was a final-year trainee teacher and responsible for a Reception class. The focus for the term was the story of *Grandpa's Vegetables*. She was keen to develop the outdoor and indoor provision so that it related to the story. Hayley placed large laminated pictures of vegetables around the outdoor area. These were accompanied with labels to show the name of each vegetable. The children were given an opportunity to follow oral or written instructions to plant vegetables in the planting area. As the vegetables grew, the children were introduced to the vocabulary of measures to enable them to compare the heights of the vegetables using language such as *tall, taller, tallest, short, shorter, shortest*. The children subsequently followed written or verbal instructions to make their own vegetable soup. In the reading area, children were introduced to other stories about fruit and vegetables including *Oliver's Vegetables* and *The Very Hungry Caterpillar*. A curiosity area was created for the children to explore a range of fruits and vegetables. This was supported with simple text which gave the children information about the food. In the workshop area, the children created their own vegetable characters using real fruits and vegetables. Photographs were taken of these characters and placed in the mark-making area. The children then worked alongside adults in the mark-making area to create their own books and captions about the characters.

- What other activities could you have planned relating to the story of *Grandpa's Vegetables*?
- What other stories could you use to facilitate a cross-curricular approach to learning while also embedding literacy skills?

INTERNATIONAL PERSPECTIVES

In Denmark literacy is frequently taught across the curriculum rather than as a discrete lesson. In England literacy is frequently taught discretely and applied across the curriculum. Which approach do you think is more beneficial to children's education?

Critical reflection

We believe in providing children with rich, varied and stimulating activities and we believe that the teaching of literacy should be embedded within a broad, rich language curriculum. We also believe that an enabling learning environment, which values language and communication and values children's emergent attempts at reading and writing, is the best way of accelerating children's achievement in literacy. However, the standards agenda and school inspections focus heavily on the quality of pupils' written outputs, and handwriting, spelling and punctuation are the hallmarks of high achievement in literacy. Inspectors value well-presented written work. This raises some critical questions.

» *To what extent does the focus on presentation lead to a devaluing of children's emergent attempts at writing?*

» *Should teachers focus on the formal skills of handwriting earlier, rather than providing opportunities for children to practise their gross motor skills through tracing letters in the air, writing with chunky chalks and writing with water and large paintbrushes?*

» *How can early years teachers present a rationale for developmentally appropriate practice which values emergent reading and writing and focuses on gross motor development before fine motor development?*

» *The Early Learning Goal at the end of the Early Years Foundation Stage states that children should be able to write simple sentences. Given this expectation, should early years practitioners focus on the formal skills of sentence structure at an earlier stage rather than focusing on developmentally appropriate practice?*

Critical points

This chapter has emphasised the importance of:

» *providing a broad and a rich language curriculum;*

» *planning an enabling learning environment which is print- and language-rich;*

» *planning for reading and writing opportunities in all areas of continuous provision;*

» *using the outdoors for planning different kinds of activities than those that can be delivered in the indoor learning environment;*

» *using working walls for demonstrating the writing process and for displaying good models of writing.*

Taking it further

Brien, J. (2012) *Teaching Primary English*. London: Sage. Chapter 9 'English and Literacy beyond the Classroom' in this book provides some useful advice on creating a language-rich environment.

11 Supporting children with literacy difficulties

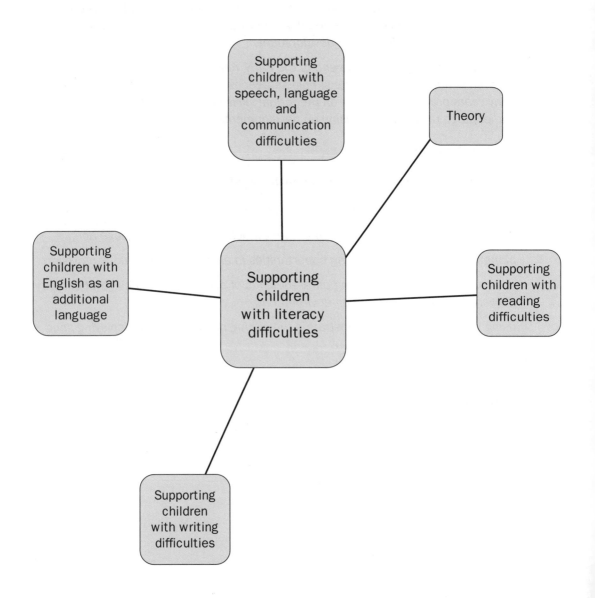

Links to the Early Years Foundation Stage

Communication and language: Listening and attention

By the end of the Early Years Foundation Stage, children need to listen attentively in a range of situations. They need to give attention to what others say and respond appropriately.

Communication and language: Understanding

During the Early Years Foundation Stage, children will begin to develop an understanding of: specific concepts such as big/little; simple prepositions such as on, under and behind; complex sentences and noun vocabulary.

Communication and language: Speaking

During the Early Years Foundation Stage children will use verbal and non-verbal communication and build up a range of vocabulary.

Literacy: Reading and writing

By the end of the Early Years Foundation Stage, children will begin to read and write simple sentences. The ability to speak and understand spoken sentences will aid the development of reading and writing.

Links to the National Curriculum

The National Curriculum identifies speaking and listening as a fundamental aspect of English. However, it is important to remember that speaking and listening opportunities should be provided across the curriculum, so speaking and listening should be viewed as tools to enable children to access the whole curriculum rather than being confined to English.

The theory

Scarborough (1990) found a correlation between early speech deficits and reading acquisition. Children who make speech errors or who experience delayed language development are more likely to experience difficulties in learning to read and may subsequently be diagnosed with dyslexia.

Supporting children with speech, language and communication difficulties

As a teacher you must acknowledge that all children will have attained varying levels in their speech, language and communication skills. You must initially be aware of the differences between speech, language and communication. The Communication Trust (2011) provides useful definitions of these terms:

Speech refers to speaking in a clear voice ... without hesitating too much or without repeating words ... and being able to make sounds ... clearly.

Language refers to talking and understanding, joining words together into sentences ... knowing the right words to explain what you mean.

Communication refers to how we interact with others, using language or gestures in different ways, for example to have a conversation or give directions. It is also being able to understand other people's points of view and understanding body language and facial expressions.

(Communication Trust, 2011)

You must remember that children communicate in a range of different ways. These may include both verbal and non-verbal forms of communication. Non-verbal communication should be valued and may include simple eye contact, gesturing or leading you to show you objects and places.

Children may encounter difficulties in either one or more of these aspects. Through careful assessments you must initially identify the specific difficulties that children are experiencing. It is only by doing so that you will be able to offer them appropriate support.

You need to consider the ways in which you can create a communication-friendly environment to support and enhance children's development. You will need to attend to the following aspects:

*   developing areas where children can engage in conversation without the distraction of noise;

*   making space available, which provides children with a chance to focus on and enjoy communication without additional distractions;

*   providing visual cues such as timetables, labels using pictures and words, stimulus displays and interactive displays, including labels and captions, and communication books to facilitate picture exchange communication.

Adults play a fundamental role in supporting the development of children's speech, language and communication skills. As children engage in learning you should seize opportunities to extend their language. As you interact with children you should scaffold their language development by introducing them to new words and phrases as well as technical vocabulary. Additionally as you plan for adult-directed teaching it is essential that you identify new vocabulary on your lesson plans. The development of vocabulary must be considered in all aspects of learning. You must note that an introduction to new vocabulary does not necessarily result in children automatically understanding and using it. Children may need to be introduced to vocabulary several times within a relevant context before they will even start to use it independently. Displaying new vocabulary is also a useful way of consolidating meaning. For example, a representation of a triangle alongside a written label can help children to make an association between a word and its meaning.

You will have responsibility for identifying children who encounter speech, language and communication difficulties. Some children will have already been referred to external agencies, while others may have been referred and discharged due to lack of parental support. Other children may not have been identified at all. Should you have any concerns about specific children and the specific support they require, we advise you to discuss this with the Special Educational Needs Co-ordinator. However, you may find the following strategies helpful.

- Simplify language and use short chunks of language to communicate meaning.

- Slow down your speech.

- Ensure that the majority of the vocabulary you use is within the child's understanding.

- Provide children with thinking time to process what has been communicated to them.

- Encourage them to echo what has been said to them.

- Ensure that a child is looking at you as you speak to them and vice versa.

- Explain in advance the information that children will be required to recall.

- Support your explanations with visual cues, including pictures, objects, diagrams and gestures.

- Demonstrate learning in tandem with your explanations. For example, when naming the parts of a flowering plant, ensure that as you identify each part you also refer to these parts on a real plant.

- Afford children time to communicate their needs and explanations without rushing them or anticipating and responding before they have had time to finish speaking. Children who stammer should not be interrupted, as this may damage their confidence and impair their willingness to communicate.

- Resist the temptation to correct children as they speak. It is advisable to repeat what they have communicated, including the correct model of spoken language, after the child has finished speaking.

- Reward children with praise for their attempts to communicate.

You cannot assume that all children will have enjoyed and adopted good communication skills. Adults around them may not have been good role models and it is your responsibility to identify this and then ensure that this becomes a focus for a child's development. The rules of communication need to be taught and modelled in one-to-one interactions with you and other colleagues. Once children become confident communicators in this context, you can extend their experiences by engaging them in opportunities to communicate with their peers on a one-to-one basis. This would be followed by communication in groups and eventually as part of the whole class. Children need to be taught explicitly the rules of communication. These include:

- good listening skills;

- allowing the speaker to finish before responding to them;

- taking turns in conversation;

- developing the skills of negotiation;

- considering the effect and impact of their communications.

The Early Years Foundation Stage guidance (DFE, 2012) provides a broad developmental framework for extending children's communication and language. You can refer to this document to support you in assessing the development of individual children as well as identifying their next developmental steps which you will then need to support. This document also provides guidance to support you in developing an enabling learning environment. A fundamental aspect of such an environment is for you to ensure that you consistently model the use of correct standard spoken English, including the correct use of grammar. As a practitioner you are a role model of standard spoken English. The standard of your own spoken and written forms of English must be exemplary. This is a current key focus in education and is embedded in the Teachers' Standards (DFE, 2012). It does not refer to regional accents, which are to be celebrated. You must be able to clearly distinguish between grammar and accent. You can speak in standard English with any accent.

CASE STUDY

Billy entered a Reception class, and assessments demonstrated that his understanding of spoken English was well below expectations in relation to his age. During one-to-one communications with adults he displayed symptoms of panic through screaming, seeking isolation and undressing himself. Initially practitioners attempted to calm him, but further communications with him only made things worse. His teacher quickly realised that Billy should be allowed to seek quiet isolation in a safe place when he needed it and be allowed the time to regain his composure. It was only at this point that the teacher would attempt to communicate with Billy. No reference was ever made to the preceding incidents. Billy was simply asked if he was feeling happy and he was helped to dress again. This was accompanied by simple conversation relating to his interests. Billy was then invited to rejoin his group of peers, and once he was calmer he usually agreed to do this. Whenever the teacher addressed the whole class to give explanations or communicate expectations, an additional adult communicated these to Billy on a one-to-one basis, simplifying the language and supporting this with modelling and gesture when deemed necessary.

- Why do you think Billy reacted in this way?

- Why did the teacher not focus on discussing Billy's behaviour with him?

- What other strategies could have been used to support Billy?

Critical questions

» *Developing children's speech, language and communication underpins children's development in reading and writing. The Early Years Foundation Stage recognises the central importance of communication and language through its identification as a prime area of learning. Is the same level of importance attached to language and communication once children enter Key Stage 1?*

» *Children with speech, language and communication difficulties often benefit from support from different agencies and parents. What are the challenges in relation to developing these partnerships?*

Supporting children with reading difficulties

While working with children you will quickly identify those who have reading difficulties. There will be many different reasons for these and it is your responsibility to quickly identify exactly what these difficulties are to enable you to address them effectively. Using the Simple View of Reading as an assessment tool is an effective way of identifying where the difficulty lies. Children experience problems with word recognition (blending/sight vocabulary) or with language comprehension or both of these skills. Once you have identified the difficulty encountered by a child, you are able to focus on planning appropriate interventions to address the challenge. When assessing children's reading it is essential that you consider the following aspects:

- phonological awareness: awareness of rhyme, alliteration, rhythm and syllables;

- an awareness of onset and rime;

- identifying a variety of units of sound within words which are precursors to subsequent phonemic awareness;

- phonemic awareness: the ability to identify and manipulate the phonemes in spoken words in sequence. This includes the ability to make grapheme–phoneme correspondences as well as blending and segmenting;

- sight word recognition: this includes sight recognition of tricky words;

- concepts about print: these include orientation of the book; understanding that print rather than pictures carries the message; direction of the print; line sequence; page sequence; the function of punctuation; and an understanding of frequently used vocabulary including *beginning*, *middle* and *end*;

- an inability to distinguish between similar graphemes, which could include 'd' and 'b' or 'g' and 'q';

- an ability to decode print but an inability to understand its meaning.

We recommend using a highly kinaesthetic approach to enable children to develop the skills of grapheme–phoneme correspondence, as well as the skills for blending and segmenting. Be aware that some children may not be ready for developing phonemic awareness because the building blocks for doing so may not be in place. In this instance you should focus on further developing children's phonological awareness.

Before children can become confident and effective readers they must have mastered the alphabetic code. This can be more challenging for some children than others and it will be necessary for you to recognise this and set the pace accordingly. Drawing on the work of Broomfield and Combley (2003), we support their approach for introducing children to grapheme–phoneme correspondences. The basic approach includes the following steps.

- *See*: children need to see both upper- and lower-case versions of the letter and to understand that both these letters share the same sound.

- *Hear*: children need to hear the sound which corresponds with the grapheme they are learning. Children must also be able to identify a sound in various positions in different words. An example of this is to identify the 'p' sound in the spoken words *pig, cap, happy*. They must note whether the sound comes at the beginning, middle or end of the word.

- *Say*: children must say the sound. To support them in doing so, the sound must be articulated correctly by the teacher.

- *Write*: children should be able to write the grapheme, using a range of media employing multi-sensory approaches.

As children begin to make grapheme–phoneme correspondences they can be introduced to blending and segmenting. Again, multi-sensory approaches should be employed. These could include introducing children to writing in glitter, in the air or with water. Children who are encountering ongoing problems with reading will need to overlearn grapheme–phoneme correspondences. Broomfield and Combley (2003) recommend daily routines which are familiar to children, including a pack of reading cards with which they practise grapheme–phoneme correspondences every day. Each reading card should include:

- upper- and lower-case versions of the letter on the front of the card;

- a word containing a clear example of the letter–sound link and a corresponding picture, on the back of the card. For example, sun/s/ with a picture of the sun.

The picture is used as a cue for the child to identify the word and then the target sound. Because children use these cards every day, their skills and confidence will grow and they will develop automatic recognition of grapheme–phoneme correspondence. It is important that children do not experience a sense of failure. This can be avoided by ensuring that when they encounter difficulties with a specific grapheme–phoneme correspondence, this is included within a group of known grapheme–phoneme correspondences. Once children have developed a bank of known grapheme–phoneme correspondences, these can be used in games such as Snap. It is important that children continue to articulate the phoneme as they see it, rather than being allowed to simply recognise the same letter shapes. This will further develop their skills and confidence.

Once a child has developed grapheme–phoneme correspondence in relation to the full alphabet, it can be helpful to present the alphabet to them as an arc. On a daily basis they can, initially, be asked to remove a given grapheme from the arc and place it underneath. Once they can confidently achieve this for all graphemes, you can engage them in selecting additional graphemes to build words underneath the alphabet arc. Each day you will focus on a specific grapheme. This will be placed in the centre of the arc and remain there throughout the lesson. All word building must relate to this grapheme. For example, if the target grapheme is 'g' the child could be asked to add further graphemes to build the words *got, rag, again, gift, flag* and *grin*. Ensure that the target words are always within a child's phonic knowledge.

Paired reading with the teacher as well as with peers can develop children's confidence with reading. A text can be shared between two people and used in a range of ways: for example, taking turns to read a page of the text while both following it, the more confident reader beginning to read the text and the other child indicating when they feel confident enough to take over the role as reader; the children may also wish to read together at the same time.

There are several other interventions available to support children who are encountering difficulties with reading. An example of one such intervention is Reading Recovery. Take care to use an intervention that appropriately meets the needs of the child you are supporting. To deliver many of these interventions requires training and it is essential that you ensure that they are accessed and delivered by trained colleagues only.

You should carefully consider your choice of texts and match these to the needs and interests of each child. Simple texts are usually suitable for young children. An older child may need to develop similar skills to his younger peers but would clearly not enjoy reading the same text. The wrong text choice can quickly result in an older child becoming disengaged from reading.

CASE STUDY

James had a profile score well below national expectations in reading at the end of the EYFS. He had good oral communication skills, he was imaginative, curious and his personal and social development was good. James loved listening to stories. He enjoyed joining in with repetitive texts. He could retell stories in the correct sequence and he could use inference to answer higher-order questions about text. Story time was his favourite time of the day. However, James disliked being the reader. From his early days in school he struggled with the concept of rhyme and alliteration as well as the identification of environmental sounds. It was evident that James was having specific difficulties with early sound discrimination and phonological awareness. The teacher decided to plan additional opportunities which focused on developing James' awareness of rhyme, alliteration, sound discrimination and early phonemic awareness. The development of these skills took several months. Throughout the intervention James was enthusiastic and enjoyed his learning but genuinely struggled with developing the pre-requisite skills for reading. By the end of the year, James had some understanding of grapheme–phoneme correspondence and was beginning to blend the phonemes in simple words for reading. However, the skills required to decode were such a challenge for him that for several months he was unable to gain any meaning from his own reading. For example, after reading a simple caption 'A black cat' James was unable to identify the animal or colour of the animal from the caption he had read.

- Why did the teacher not immediately begin to introduce graphemes and phonemes to James?

- Why could James understand more complex texts read by the teacher but not understand simple captions he had read himself?

- How might you develop simple comprehension skills with James as his decoding skills developed?

Critical questions

» *The teaching of Systematic Synthetic Phonics is now a key policy priority. Ideally all children should be able to decode confidently by the end of Key Stage 1. However, some children do not achieve this and continue to struggle with reading well into Key Stage 2. The recommendation is that these children should continue to follow a Systematic Synthetic Phonics programme. What are your views in relation to this recommendation?*

» *What are the challenges of engaging parents in supporting their child's reading development?*

CREATIVE APPROACH

In the previous case study you were introduced to James. To support his development in blending he worked with a small group of children with similar difficulties. The teacher presented herself as a witch with her cauldron. She invited the children to help her make her witch's stew. The children listened to the witch's chant:

Help me make my witch's stew. Find me the words and I'll share it with you.

Initially the teacher engaged the children in oral blending activities. She said the rhyme and then sound talked a word (for example, b-a-t) and the children were then required to locate the matching object which they had to collect and add to the stew pot. She then repeated this with different words to make up the stew. Once the children became confident with this, the objects were replaced using words accompanied by picture cues. Eventually the picture cues were removed and the children were asked to find the words.

• How could this activity be adapted to provide children with further opportunities to develop their blending skills?

• How could this activity be adapted to develop children's skills in segmenting?

Supporting children with writing difficulties

In our experience, we have found that children apply their phonic knowledge and skills to reading before they apply them to writing. Therefore we have frequently noted that children do not achieve as highly in writing as they do in reading. To address this discrepancy we advocate that they must have access to a structured writing programme. This can effectively be devised by the teacher to support children in developing the confidence and skills to apply their phonic knowledge to the writing process. You may find the following support strategies helpful.

• Model the writing process through shared writing opportunities.

• Engage children in dictation activities within the child's phonic knowledge: words, captions and sentences.

- Engage them in regular opportunities to segment words into their constituent phonemes through multi-sensory approaches: writing in sand, salt and glitter.

- Plan explicit teaching of the spelling of tricky words: this could include introducing children to the strategy of looking at the tricky word, tracing over the letters with highlighters, chalks or the finger, copying the word and finally writing it from memory. You will need to engage the children in further opportunities to read and write the tricky word. You should also make the spelling of the word a focus and address any misspellings of it in the children's independent writing. As the children read you should also draw their attention to the word as it appears within the text.

- Access alphabet mats: to support the children's independent writing.

- Access tricky-word mats: to support the children's independent writing.

- Draw on interests and experiences to ensure that the children have a clear context and purpose for writing.

- Support children with sentence structure: reassembling single words to create a sentence. This supports children in understanding the sense of a sentence.

- Engage the children in oral rehearsal before writing.

- Introducing clear writing frames will support children who are familiar with a range of genres but require support and guidance on the structural and language features of each genre. Mind maps and planning templates are useful resources.

Before writing, children must have had prior experiences on which they can draw. They must be familiar with a range of literature. Broad experiences of literature will provide them with a good foundation for taking and then adapting what they have heard, experienced and read. Drama is an effective tool for engaging children in experiencing text and cross-curricular work. Children can draw upon the ideas they have developed in drama lessons and use these in their own written work. It is important that you provide all children with positive feedback about their written work in order to engender a positive self-concept. Feedback should be focused and developmental by focusing on one specific target that the child should address in future work. Subsequent progress should be monitored against this target. In this way small steps become big strides in a child's development.

CASE STUDY

Ben had developed the ability to segment words to aid the spelling of simple words. However, his understanding of sentence structure was less well developed. He was able to speak in sentences but unable to commit these same sentences to paper. At this time in his education, he was particularly fascinated by a theme about Halloween and he enjoyed listening to stories relating to this. The teacher decided to follow Ben's interest and supported him in writing a series of stories about a witch and her friends.

The first book was entitled 'The Witch and Her Friends' and Ben's ideas were heavily supported with picture cues. The teacher showed Ben a series of pictures of animals (cat, dog, frog, bat, rat and pig) and encouraged him to select one. Ben was then asked to say what he saw, for example a pig. The teacher then echoed what Ben had said and then Ben echoed the teacher. This process was repeated several times until Ben could retain the two words (a pig) in his head. He then wrote down exactly what he had said. A new animal was then selected for each page of the book and Ben was encouraged to write the captions that he had spoken for each page.

This process introduced Ben to a clear structure for writing: *think it, say it, write it, read it*. To support him in reading the captions he had written, he was asked to work independently and reread each page and add his own illustrations to accompany the simple text. Ben began to enjoy writing simple books independently, closely following the model he had been introduced to. This provided him with security.

To develop his writing skills further, Ben worked with the teacher to write a new book in the series. On this occasion, pictures of animals were again introduced. Before Ben was shown these he was asked to focus on the colour of each animal. The story was entitled 'The Witch and Her Friends Went to the Moon'. Again he selected one illustration at a time and told the teacher what he saw, for example *a black cat*; *a red dog*. Ben was now offering extended captions of three words. He was again asked to echo the caption with the teacher to support him in remembering it. Ben was asked to write the caption and then read it and illustrate it. He then repeated this process with the other pictures to make up the book.

To extend Ben's understanding of sentence structure further, the third book in the series was entitled 'Travelling to the Moon'. Before seeing the illustrations, Ben was asked to focus on the animal, its colour and mode of transport, for example *a black cat on a mat*; *a green frog on a log*. By now Ben was familiar with the process of writing a book and he needed less prompting from the teacher. He followed the structure that he was now familiar with to complete the third book.

Ben was developing confidence as a writer, although he chose to adhere to the very tight structure that he was familiar with. He began to make small adaptations by changing the names of the animals, but this also engaged him in attempting to spell new words independently. Many of his attempts were phonetically plausible (such as *hamsta* for hamster; *gini pig* for guinea pig).

- How would you support Ben in further developing the skills to enable him to write independently?

Critical questions

» *When do you think it is important to focus on children's use of simple punctuation? Support your views.*

» *How do children's good communication, speech and language skills transfer to their writing development?*

Supporting children with English as an additional language

Children joining your class with English as an additional language will initially need to learn some key functional vocabulary. Brien (2012) recommends the following target words:

- *no*: to keep them safe;

- *toilet*: to retain personal dignity;

- *thank you*: to be liked and accepted.

Initially children may remain silent during lessons. They are simply trying to make sense of what is happening and what is being said around them. They require support from adults and children who model high standards of the use of the English language. Brien (2012) argues that they should learn alongside children with higher levels of attainment in the use of the English language and that this will more effectively support them in acquiring and using the language themselves. She therefore does not advocate placing older children, with English as an additional language, in classes with younger children. We support her views.

The following strategies may be useful in guiding you in supporting children with English as an additional language.

- Focus on the development of their speaking and listening skills: this is essential to enable them to become good readers and writers.

- Access and use visual aids: pictures and objects will give meaning to new vocabulary.

- Select dual language labels, captions and texts.

- Allow them to use oral rehearsal with talk partners before they embark on any writing activity.

- Clearly explain new vocabulary.

- Tasks may need to be shorter in duration as well as more tightly scaffolded.

- Scaffold tasks appropriately.

- Support shared reading with objects – puppets, props and pictures – to develop their understanding.

- Praise all achievements.

- Create a language-rich classroom.

Older children with English as an additional language may already have understood grapheme–phoneme correspondences in their home language and will draw upon this knowledge to develop their understanding of grapheme–phoneme correspondences in English. Their progress may be quite rapid. The sounds associated with the same graphemes may be different in English to those they have acquired in their home language and they will need to learn these. However, some languages may follow different alphabetic codes, and, for children from families who speak one of these languages, adapting to the codes to access and use English for speaking, listening, reading and writing could be more challenging.

Rose (2006) recommends the development of speaking and listening skills and vocabulary building as essential features of high-quality provision for children with English as an additional language. He also advocates immersing them in opportunities for talking about and sharing their own cultural experiences as well as encouraging them to engage with traditional texts from their own cultures. He advocates the use of a Systematic Synthetic Phonics approach to support reading, as evidence suggests that this is an equally successful approach for English-speaking children as well as their peers with English as an additional language.

CASE STUDY

Aleksy had recently joined a Reception class from Eastern Europe. He had been in the school for one month and had no understanding of the English language on arrival. Within this very short space of time he had quickly developed an understanding of grapheme–phoneme correspondence and he was able to articulate several phonemes in response to their corresponding graphemes. This was facilitated through multi-sensory approaches within the daily phonics lesson as well as additional individual support. He enjoyed working with adults and children in shared reading and writing experiences. Very quickly he developed the skills of blending and segmenting and he was able to read and write simple words. These experiences were reinforced through multi-sensory approaches. The teacher supported his understanding of simple words with pictures to introduce him to some key vocabulary within the scope of his existing phonic knowledge. Aleksy quickly enjoyed writing freely. He developed an understanding of several concepts about print and he frequently and independently wrote a series of non-words from left to right, which included a space between each word. He proudly and confidently shared these with the adults and was able to read back what he had written using his blending skills.

Critical questions

» *Do you think it is appropriate to introduce children with English as an additional language to non-words?*

» *In the above case study, Aleksy participated in the Year 1 phonics screening test in 2012. He was significantly more successful than some of his English-speaking peers, whose levels of attainment in reading were significantly higher than those demonstrated by Aleksy. Why do you think Aleksy achieved more highly than some of his peers on the screening test?*

» *Does this indicate that Aleksy is a better reader than some of his peers?*

Critical reflection

The current standards agenda in education focuses on the need for all schools to maximise levels of achievement and attainment for all pupils in reading and writing.

» *How does this impact on schools that have high proportions of children with special educational needs or high proportions of second language learners?*

» *What is the impact of the standards agenda on schools that work with children who come from language- and literacy-impoverished home environments?*

» *How would you overcome the challenge of engaging children who have not acquired language in the reading and writing process?*

» *Policy initiatives in recent years have strongly advocated the development of school–parent partnerships to enhance achievement. How could you address the challenge of supporting children whose parents are illiterate?*

Critical points

This chapter has emphasised the importance of:

» *identifying children's difficulties in communication, language and literacy early;*

» *strategies for supporting children who display such difficulties;*

» *developing a communication-friendly environment;*

» *a multi-sensory approach for supporting children's reading and writing difficulties;*

» *structuring writing tasks so that children experience a sense of success.*

Taking it further

Bryant, P. and Bradley, L. (1985) *Children's Reading Problems*. Oxford: Blackwell.

12 Assessing English in the early years

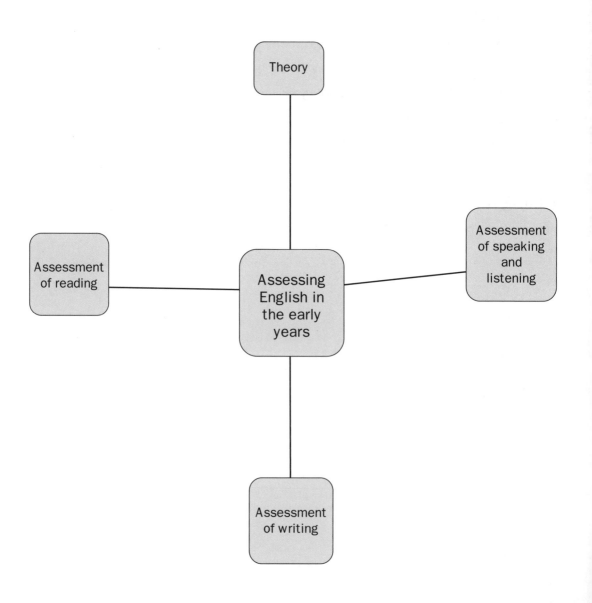

Links to the Early Years Foundation Stage

The Development Matters statements in the Early Years Foundation Stage support formative assessment. The Early Years Foundation Stage profile supports summative assessment judgements.

Links to the National Curriculum

National Curriculum level descriptors are specified for children in Key Stages 1 and 2. These demonstrate what achievement in reading, writing, speaking and listening looks like at different levels.

The theory

Formative assessment is an ongoing process which supports the identification of short-term learning needs. It informs future planning on a daily basis and takes place within and between lessons. It is usually informal and reflects the independent knowledge, skills and understanding of each child. Its purpose is to support teaching and learning to meet the specific needs of individuals, groups of learners and whole classes.

Summative assessment is a summary of a child's achievements over a specified period of time. It can take place after a unit of work, at the end of a half term or at the end of a key stage. It can be formal or informal and usually leads to the identification of broad targets to support children's development. The outcomes are usually expressed in quantitative terms. It serves as an accountability tool for teachers and schools, as the outcomes of summative assessment are transmitted to head teachers, local authorities and parents, and outcomes at the end of key stages are reported to the government.

Black and Wiliam (1998) found that formative assessment was the most effective way of raising standards.

Assessment of speaking and listening

There are national level descriptors for assessing children's speaking and listening in Key Stages 1 and 2, and your school will have adopted non-statutory criteria which break down each broad level into high, medium and low. In the Early Years Foundation Stage, assessments are divided between listening and attention and the separate aspect of speaking. The Early Years Foundation Stage profile will support you in assessing children's development in these areas.

An assessment of children's speaking and listening skills can be conducted during planned speaking activities and child-initiated learning. You can assess their speaking and listening skills not just in literacy but also across the curriculum. Children need to be taught the skills of speaking and listening through planned activities which demonstrate progression over time. If you do not plan a speaking and listening curriculum, children will not be given a fair opportunity to demonstrate their skills.

Assessment of reading

Children's early development in reading often begins at home as they are introduced to stories and rhymes by their parents and carers. As a teacher it is essential that you involve parents and carers in initial and ongoing assessments of reading. As you observe children, your assessments should indicate whether they:

- enjoy books and other printed materials;

- handle books and printed materials with interest;

- have favourite books and rhymes;

- repeat words or phrases from familiar stories;

- look at books independently;

- handle books carefully;

- know that print carries information;

- hold books the correct way up and turn the pages;

- know that print is read from left to right and top to bottom;

- join in with repeated refrains;

- suggest how the story might end;

- join in with stories one-to-one or in small groups;

- show an awareness of rhyme and alliteration.

By the end of the Foundation Stage, children are expected to be able to decode simple regular words and read some common irregular words. It is an expectation that they will be able to read simple sentences and have some understanding of what they have read. Your observations should identify whether children can blend the phonemes all the way through a word to support them in reading the word. Initially, in reading, the focus of your assessments will be on children's ability to decode text and to recognise some words by sight. Without these skills they will never be able to gather meaning from what they have read. As children become more fluent readers the focus of your assessments will subsequently include their ability to gain understanding from the text. Initially you will ask children to communicate information that can be directly retrieved from the text they have read. As children become fluent readers, your assessments will subsequently focus on their ability to use the skills of inference and deduction to answer higher-order questions about the text.

The skills of decoding and comprehension are developed concurrently. The Simple View of Reading provides a useful conceptual framework upon which to base your assessments of children's reading development. According to this conceptual framework, reading is the product of both word recognition and language comprehension processes. However, as a teacher of young children you would initially place more emphasis on the skill of decoding. If children are unable to decode text, they will clearly be unable to read the words on a page and this will prevent them from gaining understanding of the print.

However, initially, when the main focus of your teaching is the skill of decoding, you must not neglect the opportunities to develop children's understanding that both print and language convey meaning. This should be facilitated through access to a broad and rich language curriculum which will enable you to assess children's language comprehension skills. Access to story time, a print-rich environment, speaking and listening and role play provide children with opportunities to use and understand language in different contexts. It is your role to extend children's understanding of language through a range of planned and incidental interactions with young children. As children become more confident with decoding, you can start to assess their ability to retrieve simple information directly from the text, as well as their ability to recognise the words on the page.

Decoding is a time-limited skill, and once children are reading fluently the focus of your assessments will need to include a greater emphasis on children's ability to understand the text. In relation to fiction or poetry your assessments might focus on children's ability to:

- name characters;
- identify settings;
- recall events;
- sequence events;
- describe and talk about characters;
- identify morals;
- compare different versions of a story;
- predict subsequent events;
- discuss word and language choices and the intended impact.

In relation to non-fiction texts your assessments will indicate whether children can:

- retrieve factual information from the text;
- use organisational/presentational devices including the contents page, index, tables, charts and glossaries.

We suggest that individual reading conferences with children provide you with the most effective means of assessing children's word recognition and language comprehension skills. The Simple View of Reading will enable you to identify whether children are strong or weak in both skills or are stronger in one skill than in the other. To be good readers, children need to be strong in both word recognition and language comprehension. By assessing children in relation to each skill you can then provide specific tailored intervention in relation to the deficit skill(s). It is important to recognise that a poor reader can require support in either word recognition, language comprehension or both of these skills. Some children are very adept at decoding text but may have limited understanding of language and/or text. These children will require additional intervention in the area of language comprehension rather than additional intervention in word recognition. Assessing each child in your class in relation to the two skills in the Simple View of Reading will enable you to identify individuals or groups of children requiring additional support in these skills. Simply acknowledging that a child is a poor reader will not enable you to offer specific tailored intervention. You need to know why the child finds reading difficult.

In addition to individual assessments you can also track the performance of groups of readers of similar abilities through group assessments conducted during guided reading sessions. This will enable you to identify the next steps for specific groups of children. However, as reading is a very individual process, we maintain that individual reading conferences provide the best means of teaching and assessing reading. In our experience, groups of readers for guided reading are deemed to have similar learning needs based on similar levels of attainment. An example of this would be the identification of a guided reading group where all the children are working within level 2c. The assumption can be that they have shared learning needs based on the level they have achieved. In reality, their learning needs in reading may differ greatly because children may be assessed at level 2c for different reasons.

Critical question

»   *Some schools only teach and assess reading through a guided group approach (guided reading). Do you agree with this?*

Assessment of writing

The Early Years Foundation Stage profile will support you in assessing the writing development of young children. By the end of this phase, children should be able to write simple irregular words and make phonetically plausible attempts to spell new words. Additionally they should be able to write simple sentences. The National Curriculum specifies level descriptors for children in Key Stages 1 and 2. Children working at level 1 are able to demonstrate that they can use writing to communicate meaning. For those working at level 2 their writing will demonstrate a greater awareness of punctuation and the use of a wider range of vocabulary. However, it is helpful to break each level down further in order to track pupils' progress more effectively into low, secure and high. A range of assessment tools have been developed by schools, local authorities and the National Strategies for this purpose. One example of such a tool is *Assessing Pupils' Progress* (APP) which was developed by the National Strategies.

Making a judgement about children's writing is challenging. It is more effective to look at a range of writing produced by each child and then to make a judgement on the basis of several pieces of work rather than against one piece of work. Initially, we recommend that you read the work with your mentor and then together look at the assessment criteria to see which level 'best fits' that piece of work. Ultimately this is not an exact science and the final judgement will be a 'best fit' judgement. Your school may have developed a portfolio of writing assessed at different levels and this might be useful as a basis for benchmarking the work against. There are no nationally agreed assessment criteria for what constitutes high, medium or low performance at a specific level. However, the assessment criteria used by your school will specify criteria which you should base your judgements upon.

Children should be able to assess their own performance in writing. Some schools have developed child-friendly criteria in order to aid pupil self-assessment. We recommend that you highlight the criteria that children have met and this will enable you to use the criteria that are not highlighted for identifying their next steps. Children should also be able to identify their personal targets using child-friendly versions of the criteria. We also recommend that you hold regular writing conferences with children where they review their progress in their writing and identify targets for further development with you. As a teacher you should aim to review children's writing with the child every half term.

In terms of assessing their progress within lessons, children will be able to self-assess their own writing if you make it really clear what you are looking for in their work. If they know that you want them to use imperative verbs in their instructional writing they can then assess their writing when it is completed to see if they have done it. Peer assessment is also a useful assessment method and this enables children to give each other feedback about what they have done well (*what went well* – 'WWW') and ways of making the work better (*even better if* – 'EBI').

Critical question

» *There is a key focus placed on individual achievement in reading and writing. What do you consider to be the benefits of equally robust assessments in the area of speaking and listening?*

CREATIVE APPROACH

Children should identify their targets in consultation with you. These should be clearly visible to the child to enable them to measure and identify their own progress. Targets should be measurable and achievable to ensure that children enjoy success.

CASE STUDY

Yasmin entered a Year 1 class with an individual education plan to support her in making further progress in reading and writing. All targets identified on the plan related directly to either reading or writing. Through formative assessment her new teacher quickly identified that Yasmin had under-developed speaking and listening skills and that she struggled to understand more complex language. Additionally, her attention skills were poor. These combined factors were clearly impacting negatively on Yasmin's progress in reading and writing. Her parents were consulted and new targets were identified which focused on developing Yasmin's understanding and use of language as well as her listening and attention skills.

* Why did the teacher replace the reading and writing targets with new targets?

Critical reflection

Accurate formative assessment enables you to identify children's current achievements and next steps in learning. To do this successfully assessment must

be integral to your classroom practice rather than being an additional 'bolt-on' task. How is formative assessment more beneficial to the teacher and child than summative assessment?

Critical points

This chapter has emphasised the importance of:

» *making assessment integral to your daily teaching;*

» *involving the child in the assessment process to enable them to identify their own achievements and next steps in learning;*

» *the relationship between speaking and listening, reading and writing;*

» *formative assessment in shaping and supporting teaching and learning.*

Taking it further

Johnson, R. and Watson, J. (2007) *Teaching Synthetic Phonics.* Exeter: Learning Matters. Chapter 8 provides useful guidance on how to assess and diagnose reading problems.

Conclusion

Throughout this book we have emphasised the importance of Systematic Synthetic Phonics and its importance in reading and writing. We believe that a systematic approach to phonics will enable the majority of children to decode text using blending as the prime approach. In turn, the ability to segment words into their constituent phonemes facilitates the development of spelling and this enables children to become independent writers.

We have stressed that blending should be time-limited and that, once it is mastered, children can more fully develop the equally important skills of comprehension. The Simple View of Reading visually demonstrates that both word recognition and language comprehension are essential for the development of effective reading. You should focus on both aspects right from the start. However, in the initial stages of reading development, decoding will be a key focus in your teaching. As children develop increased fluency in their reading, it is essential to focus your teaching on the development of reading comprehension strategies. As with blending, comprehension strategies must be taught. They are not simply acquired by children.

There may of course be some children who do not make the expected progress in word recognition by the end of Key Stage 1. You should keep rigorous assessments of all children in order to identify specific learners requiring further challenge and specific intervention. These children will benefit greatly from a systematic approach to synthetic phonics in Key Stage 2. However, children cannot just be given 'more of the same'. They may benefit from a more structured approach which operates at a slower pace.

Our view is that Systematic Synthetic Phonics will not provide all the tools that a child needs to become a reader or writer. We support Jim Rose's recommendation that a systematic approach to synthetic phonics needs to take place within the context of a broad and rich language curriculum. Children need opportunities to read a range of texts and they need to be presented with opportunities to read for pleasure. The more children read, the better their reading will become. Reading for pleasure enhances vocabulary and exposes children to a wide range of ideas which they can draw upon in their own writing. Although decodable texts are necessary in the early stages of reading, in isolation they will not provide children with all the tools they need to become effective readers and writers. We support the current focus on introducing children to a wide range of authors, poets, stories, poems and non-fiction texts because children need access to the full range of text types.

Systematic Synthetic Phonics is one tool within the toolkit for developing readers and writers. It needs to be taught in a creative way and within the context of a broad and rich language and literacy curriculum. Children need rich opportunities to work alongside recognised authors and poets and they need to orally rehearse their writing before they commit their ideas to paper. Children need to be provided with opportunities to publish their work in a variety of forms, and speaking and listening need to be valued in the same way that reading and writing are emphasised. We hope that this text has inspired you to experiment with creative approaches to support your teaching. It does not tell you everything you need to know and it will not answer all your questions. However, it adds to the already extensive body of material that has previously been published on primary English. If it helps you to deliver good and outstanding teaching then it has been a worthwhile endeavour.

References

Black, P. and Wiliam, D. (1998) *Inside the Black Box: Raising Standards through Classroom Assessment.* Windsor: NFER.

Bradley, L. and Bryant, P.E. (1983) Categorising Sounds and Learning to Read – A Causal Connection. *Nature*, 301: 419–421.

Bradley, L. and Bryant, P.E. (1985) *Rhyme and Reason in Reading and Spelling.* (*I.A.R.L.D Monographs*, 1.) Ann Arbor: University of Michigan Press.

Brien, J. (2012) *Teaching Primary English*. London: Sage.

Broomfield, H. and Combley, M. (2003) *Overcoming Dyslexia: A Practical Handbook for the Classroom*. London: Whurr Publishers.

Bruce, T. and Spratt, J. (2008) *Essentials of Literacy from 0–7: A Whole-Child Approach to Communication, Language and Literacy*. London: Sage.

Bryant, P., MacLean, M. and Bradley, L. (1990) Rhyme, Language and Children's Reading. *Applied Psycholinguistics*, 11: 237–252.

Bryant, P.E., MacLean, M., Bradley, L. and Crossland, J. (1990) Rhyme and Alliteration, Phoneme Detection and Learning to Read. *Developmental Psychology*, 26, (3): 429–438.

Burns, E. and Bell, S. (2010) Voices of Teachers with Dyslexia in Finnish and English Further and Higher Educational Settings. *Teachers and Teaching: Theory and Practice*, 16, (5): 529–543.

Burns, E. and Bell, S. (2011) Narrative Construction of Professional Teacher Identity of Teachers with Dyslexia. *Teachers and Teaching: Theory and Practice*, 27: 952–960.

Department for Education (DFE) (2011) *Criteria for Assuring High-Quality Phonic Work*. Runcorn: DFE.

Department for Education (DFE) (2012a) *Development Matters in the Early Years Foundation Stage*. London: DFE.

Department for Education (DFE) (2012b) *Teachers' Standards in England*. London: DFE.

Department for Education and Employment (DFEE) (1998) *The National Literacy Strategy: Framework for Teaching*. London, DFEE.

Department for Education and Skills (DFES) (2007) *Letters and Sounds*. London: DFES.

Ehri, L.C. (1995) Phases of Development in Learning to Read Words by Sight. *Journal of Research in Reading*, 18, (2): 116–125.

Ellis, N. and Large, B. (1987) The Development of Reading: As You Seek so Shall You Find. *British Journal of Psychology*, 78: 1–28.

Goswami, U. (1986) Children's Use of Analogy in Learning to Read: A Developmental Study. *Journal of Experimental Child Psychology*, 42: 73–83.

Goswami, U. (1988) Children's Use of Analogy in Learning to Spell. *British Journal of Developmental Psychology*, 6: 21–33.

Goswami, U. and Bryant, P. (2010) Children's Cognitive Development and Learning, in Alexander, R. (ed) *The Cambridge Primary Review Research Surveys*. Abingdon: Routledge.

Gough, P.B. and Tunmer, W.E. (1986) Decoding, Reading and Reading Disability. *Remedial Special Education*, 7: 6–10.

Griffiths, S. (2012) 'Being Dyslexic Doesn't Make Me Less of a Teacher'. School Placement Experiences of Student Teachers with Dyslexia: Strengths, Challenges and a Model for Support. *Journal of Research in Special Educational Needs*, 12, (2): 54–65.

Henderson, E. (1985) *Teaching Spelling*. Boston: Houghton Mifflin.

MacLean, M., Bryant, P.E. and Bradley, L. (1987) Rhymes, Nursery Rhymes and Reading in Early Childhood. *Merrill-Palmer Quarterly*, 33: 255–282.

Muter, V., Hulme, C., Snowling, M. J. and Stevenson, J. (2004) Phonemes, Rimes, Vocabulary and Grammatical Skills as Foundations of Early Reading Development: Evidence from a Longitudinal Study. *Developmental Psychology*, 40, (5): 665–681.

Nicholls, J., Bauers, A., Pettitt, D., Redgwell, V., Seaman, E. and Watson, G. (1989) *Beginning Writing*. Milton Keynes: Open University Press.

Ofsted (2010) *Reading by Six: How the Best Schools do it*. Ofsted.

Ofsted (2012a) *Moving English Forward: Action to Raise Standards in English*. Ofsted.

Ofsted (2012b) *From Training to Teaching Early Language and Literacy*. Ofsted.

Palaiologou, I. (2010) Communication, Language and Literacy, in Palaiologou, I (ed) *The Early Years Foundation Stage: Theory and Practice*, 138–152. London: Sage.

Riddick, B. (2001) Dyslexia and Inclusion: Time for a Social Model of Disability Perspective. *International Studies in Sociology of Education*, 11, (3): 223–236.

Riddick, B. (2003) Experiences of Teachers and Trainee Teachers Who Are Dyslexic. *International Journal of Inclusive Education*, 7, (4): 389–402.

Rose, J. (2006) *Independent Review of the Teaching of Early Reading*. Nottingham: DFES.

Scarborough, H.S. (1990) Very Early Language Deficits in Dyslexic Children. *Child Development*, 61: 1728–1743.

Sulzby, E. and Teale, W.H. (1991) Emergent Literacy, in Barr, R., Kamil, M.L., Mosenthal, P. and Pearson, D. (eds) *Handbook of Reading Research*, vol 2. White Plains, NY: Longman, 727–758.

Whitehead, M. (1999) *Supporting Language and Literacy Development in the Early Years*. Buckingham: Open University Press.

Glossary

Adjacent consonants

Adjacent consonants appear next to each other in words, eg *flag*, *sprint*. They are also known as consonant clusters. In synthetic phonics, each consonant within a cluster represents a phoneme.

Alliteration

Within a sentence or caption each word begins with the same sound, eg *sizzling sausages sound silly*.

Alphabetic code

The sounds of our language are represented by letters. In English there are approximately 44 sounds. However, there are only 26 letters of the alphabet, so we sometimes have to use more than one letter to represent a sound. These are called graphemes.

Analytic phonics

This approach does not use the smallest units of sound. In the words *cat*, *mat*, *hat*, *sat* children are introduced to the common unit of sound 'at'. This is called the rime. The consonant preceding the vowel is called the onset.

Blending

In synthetic phonics, blending is the prime approach through which children read an unknown word. It is the process of identifying the constituent phonemes represented by each grapheme within a word. Children work through the word systematically from left to right identifying each phoneme in turn. They merge these together to identify the target word.

Consonant digraph

Two consonants represent one phoneme, eg <u>ch</u>ip, <u>sh</u>ip, <u>th</u>ink.

Digraph

Two letters make one phoneme, eg ri<u>ch</u>, <u>rai</u>n, f<u>ee</u>t, b<u>oa</u>t, thr<u>oa</u>t. Vowel digraphs are made up of two vowels, and consonant digraphs are represented by two consonants.

Grapheme

A grapheme is the written representation of the phoneme. There are approximately 44 phonemes in the English language, and each phoneme is represented by a grapheme. Graphemes can be made up of one letter or more than one letter. There are always the same number of phonemes and graphemes in a word. Some graphemes can represent different phonemes, eg the 'ch' in *chip*, *chemist* or *champagne*. The same phoneme can also be represented by different graphemes, eg the /s/ phoneme in *sun* (represented by 's') and *palace* (represented by the grapheme 'ce').

Grapheme–phoneme correspondence

When we make a grapheme–phoneme correspondence we look at a specific grapheme and say the corresponding phoneme (sound).

Onset

This is the part of the word that comes before the vowel, eg *fl*ip, *cl*ap, *sn*ow. In analytic phonics these are taught as digraphs, but in synthetic phonics each separate consonant represents a phoneme, eg /f/l/a/g/.

Phoneme

A phoneme is the smallest unit of meaningful sound in a word. In English there are approximately 44 phonemes (or sounds of speech).

Phonemic awareness

This refers to the ability to detect the phonemes within a spoken word and to manipulate them.

Phonological awareness

This refers to the ability to detect the sounds within a spoken word and to manipulate them. It includes phonemes, but also the ability to detect larger sound units such as syllables and rimes.

Rime

The rime is the vowel and the rest of the syllable in a word, eg in *cup* the rime is /up/.

Segmentation

The process of segmentation refers to the ability to hear the individual phonemes within a given word. It can be done orally initially when children say out loud the individual phonemes in a given word. Children learn to represent the phonemes that they can hear with graphemes. Segmentation becomes an approach to aid spelling.

Tricky word

These are words which are not phonetically regular. It is unhelpful to sound them out. They include words such as *said* or *the*.

Trigraph

In a trigraph three letters represent one phoneme, eg l<u>igh</u>t, f<u>air</u> or f<u>ear</u>.

Vowel digraph

In a vowel digraph two vowels combine to represent one phoneme, eg b<u>oa</u>t. In a split vowel digraph the vowel digraph is split with a consonant, eg in the word c<u>a</u>k<u>e</u>.

Index